Good Grief

God's Sustaining Presence

during My Heartbreak

David A. Dean

HIMES Publications
Live Oak, Florida
- 2012 -

ISBN 0-913439-09-6

Copyright © 2012 by David Arnold Dean

Published by HIMES PUBLICATIONS,

10432 233rd Road, Live Oak, Florida 32060

Photo on back cover by LifeTouch, Galion, OH, and used
by permission.

Cover design by Sarah Wortham.

Printed in the United States of America

Acknowledgments

The Advent Christian Village at Dowling Park (Florida's oldest retirement community) has been my home since 1996. It brightened my wife's closing years and surrounded me with love and comfort after her death. I only wish I could adequately convey my gratitude for the compassion of the village administrators, its church and pastoral staff, plus all our friends and neighbors.

Their kindness followed on the heels of the gracious hospitality and housing that Rev. and Mrs. Lee Welkley provided us while my family and I were so far from home during Dottie's final hospitalization. My Men's Bible Class here stood by me during my bereavement, encouraged me to continue my teaching, and enabled this volume through their gifts. Thanks to the past and present members for showing me what fellowship among men can become.

Rev. Paul Bertolino (on whose pastoral staff I was serving as associate at McAlpin, Florida) was my guide and closest friend during my earliest days in the shadows of sadness. My thanks also to Ms. Barbara. May God bless this entire community as generously as he has enriched me through you.

More directly related to this book, I thank the editors of our village's annual literary journal for permission to reprint the revision of an article included originally in Village Voices 2011. It appears as chapter 22 in this volume.

My debt to Karen of KarenWattsBooks.com is far greater than she may ever know. Her interest and encouragement came when I needed them most. Without her I have no idea where I would have found the second wind needed to push this task to completion.

When pastor and author Clayton Blackstone volunteered his counsel and editorial assistance, I'm afraid he never dreamed how hard he would have to work. But now he can rest, and I can take credit for how much I learned from one of my former students.

Thanks also to my friend, former faculty colleague, and editor of Henceforth Publications, Dr. Freeman Barton, who has enabled the joint publication and distribution of this volume. It's an honor to work with you once again, Freeman.

God has blessed me with many friends and comforters and encouragers. Although I cannot list you individually, I am grateful that you channeled God's blessing into my life and enabled me to share my story of the Lord's faithfulness.

Contents

Foreword

In his classic and ground-breaking study on grief written in 1944 Erich Lindemann, referred to the pattern of the symptoms of grief by stating, "The picture shown by persons in acute grief is remarkably uniform." He is, of course, referencing the effects on respiration such as sighing, the feelings of severe exhaustion, the digestive upsets, the strange visualizations, the tendencies toward guilt feelings, and the sense of loss of warmth toward others. Yet we are struck almost seven decades later with how little uniformity exists in the broad manner by which people grieve. The manifestations of our sorrow in the face of profound personal loss seem to be as richly variegated as personality itself. The reason is self-evident: the experience is so intensely personal it must inevitably be reflective of our uniqueness built upon genetic structure, personality, experiences, beliefs, values, etc.

We have learned by experience that grief is a blend of emotions related to some notable distress, usually a significant loss. We know that the grieving person is likely experiencing a combination of different feelings such as sadness, emptiness, hurt, confusion, frustration, anger, fear, or a number of other possible emotions. We have all been there—or we will be!

Second, we have learned that grief has much to do with the progression or journey that must occur subsequent to some painful bereavement or loss.

Following the death of his wife, Joy Davidman, C. S. Lewis chronicled his own pathway through the process of grief:

I thought I could describe a state; make a map of sorrow. Sorrow, however, turns out to be not a state but a process, it needs not a map but a history, and if I don't stop writing that history at some quite arbitrary point, there's no reason why I should ever stop. There is something new to be chronicled every day. Grief is like a long valley, a winding valley where any bend may reveal a totally new landscape. As I've already noted, not every bend does. Sometimes the surprise is the opposite one; you are presented with exactly the same sort of country you thought you left behind miles ago. That is when you wonder whether the valley isn't a circular trench. But it isn't. There are partial recurrences, but the sequence doesn't repeat. (A Grief Observed 68-69)

What we are blessed with, in this rare glimpse into the heart and mind of Dr. David A. Dean, is a rich understanding of what it is truly like to tread that long, lonesome valley. While our grieving is uniquely our own, we can be immeasurably enriched by human experience keenly observed, insightfully reflected, and artfully preserved. Dr. Dean allows us to first comprehend a marital relationship that lived up to the nobility of divine expectation: rich in faith-based mission, shared hopes and dreams, and ever-deepening companionship. Into that warm and trusting bond intruded suddenly a mortal illness upon the one who was ironically preparing for the loss of her partner. David was understandably stunned. He sat by the bedside of his dying wife and realized she had grown old and he hadn't even noticed. Consider his words

> Looking back, I suspect that deep within me the grief was already dawning that in a few more hours would crush my spirit. I knew as well as anyone that old people die. I now realized that my wife was in that group. She was dying. So my acknowledging her as old actually became God's way of showing me that Dorothy Pierce and David Dean would soon complete their vows of lifelong faithfulness to each other.

With unwavering honesty, a perceptive eye, and a writer's gift Dr. Dean permits us to journey with him through the predictable stages of grief such as being preoccupied with his beloved Dottie and his recurring tendency to feel guilty for the little things he could have done to show her how much he adored her. Along the pathway he discovers that grief is not ever-present. Rather, it tends to come when he least expects it in what he terms "grief attacks." His efforts to balance out a reasonable disposition of her possessions

with retaining those that hold inherent memories and senti-
mental value provide a useful frame of reference for other
men who may tragically lose their wives. Observe both his
guilt and his remarkable insight into his emotional turmoil
in the following passage about Dottie's baskets.

My guilt over banishing the baskets may sound ridiculous to you (as it does to me in looking back). But
my sorrow was showing me its ability to produce guilt.
And these baskets are perhaps only one of many instances of grief producing an unmerited sense of guilt.
The arrival of death in our home has reminded me of
what I have observed over the years. Grief intertwines
with closely related destructive emotions, like guilt, anger, and depression. But guilt knows how to torment me
with a long series of doubt-raising questions. Had I really been thoughtful and loving to my wife over the years
of our marriage?

With a thoughtful approach to every facet of the journey
Dr. Dean blazes a trail for all men who find themselves in
similar circumstances. For a number of obvious and some
not so obvious reasons men do not fare as well with the loss
of a spouse as women. Dr. Dean provides a template for how
to deliberately vary routine and find "a new normal." He is
very intentional and strategic about how he works to keep
his children coordinated in a mutually supportive family circle of sojourneying grievers. He offers by his example useful
strategies for approaching those holidays and anniversaries
that can be almost devastating for the newly bereaved. This
personal journal has become a rare treasure for widowers

everywhere, filling a long unfilled void. Finally, men have an authentic and transparent standard by which to measure and reflect upon their own similar yet unique bereavement and a model for sincere exploration of their own inner pain and turmoil. This personal account is a must read for any man of faith who has suddenly been faced with the loss of his cherished beloved.

The most critical modeling that Dr. David A. Dean provides on his journey through the valley of grief is the resurrection hope that derives from his deep-seated faith he shared with his beloved wife, Dorothy. That faith which sustained them in their life together is now the core of his hope that they will one day be reunited and resume their interrupted relationship. In the beginning he held firmly to the verse from Job 1:21 "The Lord gave and the Lord has taken away; may the name of the Lord be praised." He carried on with the prayer: "I thank you, Lord, for every year you gave me with Dorothy, and I thank you for your continued presence in my life without her." But ultimately he found his greatest strength in knowing that we sorrow not as others who have no hope. He is absolutely steadfast in biblical conviction that gives rise to a blessed hope they both shared. One glorious day the trumpet will sound, the clouds will be rolled back as a scroll, the Lord shall descend, the dead in Christ shall rise, and Dorothy Pierce and David Dean will be back together once again!

--**Sidney L. Bradley, Ph.D**, Pastoral Counselor, Foresthill Church, Charlotte, N. C.

Preface

Any author ought to know what's he's writing about and for whom. Well, I know that I've been writing about my experiences since my wife died. But I'm still not sure just who I have been writing for. I don't know whether I have written this volume for you or for me. And here's why.

After my wife's death God sent me friends who encouraged me to talk about her and about my own sense of loss. And did I ever need to talk! My sadness did not feel as I expected. I was confused about my emotions. I didn't know how I ought to act. I longed to locate a book in which some widower shared his experience. I needed some guidance. When I complained that I couldn't find that kind of volume, a friend urged me to write out my own chronicle of sorrow. Being much too upset to write about anything I quickly shrugged off the possibility.

Yet I sensed he was on to something. I needed to sort out my feelings, which writing often helps me to do. I also needed to think through how I should react to my grief. Again the process of committing ideas to paper clarifies situations for me. Maybe I could step back from the turmoil, look at my mourning, and write about it. So I attempted several brief articles dealing with specific happenings and my response to them. This forced me to consider the sequence of events and their effects. Clearly in these first few articles I was writing for my own benefit.

If my children appeared in my accounts I sent them copies, and they in turn shared these with others. I soon found some of them contacting me to compare their grief to mine. Their responses encouraged me to take more literary snap shots of my own progress, but now to see if there were more similarities along our trails of sorrow. Perhaps reports of my struggles might further assist and even guide others in adjusting to their new status. My concern was expanding beyond myself to include others. Almost before I knew it I was accepting my friend's challenge until my work included all these pages. Making and assembling the pictures in my "Grief Album" has been good for me. It has forced me to face up to my feelings and to search for their meaning. It has kept Dorothy in my thoughts and has encouraged me to shed the tears which lead to healing. I hope that as you thumb through these word pictures you also will be helped by discovering the common elements in our experiences.

At the same time, realize that you are holding only a partial record of how I have experienced sorrow. This is my story. If you have mourned the death of a loved one you will find some elements that are familiar to you. You may also notice significant differences between your narrative and mine. Sorrow is a universal emotion; every normal person will have it. But since we are all different, no two of us will feel it at the same points, or with the same intensity, or have the same reactions.

Initially I was confused because I was unsure which of the common grief experiences I would share and which might not hit me. Nor can you foreknow as you face a time of sorrow. You may already have shared many of my feelings and responses; but, some of your trials will be far different. I urge you to live through your own grief. Do not worry, as I did, about what others may think. Sorrow in your own way. Do not be surprised by the feelings you have.

These pages introduce you to how grief may behave by showing how it has affected one other person. In that case you can know that someone else understands how you feel. However, if some of my trials are different from yours, be thankful for what you have been spared and prepare for others that I have not had. In either case, may you find as I did the faithfulness of the God of all Comfort, who—whether we sense it or not—is with us in our valley of darkest shadows.

I have walked this path now for over a year on a journey that has slowly become easier. I began recording it for my own benefit and ended up hoping that it might also help you. I guess the telling of my story in this form is for both of us

I dare not assume my grieving is over, for sadness does not let us go so easily. And I do not doubt those who have been this way before when they tell me that, "You never get over it." Still I can testify that the Lord has been with me all the way, and I offer my experiences as evidence.

And I invite any who mourn to join me in placing your confidence in a Good Shepherd who will never leave nor forsake us in whatever yet lies ahead.

David A. Dean

February 28, 2012   Dowling Park, Florida

Part One

Beginning of My Sorrows: Month One

*T*hough I sensed it was impending, I was stunned when my wife breathed her last. What I had known as inevitable now became real, but was too unbelievable to accept. With the gradual dawning of the truth my personal world started to crumble. The many things I needed to do confronted me. Yet only a part of me was left to do them. So began my sorrows. Confusion is the word most adequate to summarize those early days. Incoming phone calls interrupted my attempts to notify others of her death. Urgent questions from unexpected sources broke in on my time with friends who came to console us. Everything needed to be done at once: conferences with clergy, funeral director, florists; coordinating travel details and housing for my family; locating needed documents; retelling the sad story for newcomers. It seemed that no decisions could be made until others had been made first. Everything cried out for immediate attention while my personal anguish prevented me from thinking straight. I wanted the whole upheaval just to go away. My sorrow intensified when I first retired to an empty bed. It compounded as I notified other family and friends and decided details for the funeral. Talking incessantly about my wife didn't ease my sorrow; but being unable to talk to her intensified it. Meanwhile, sorting through her personal things further broke my heart.

1. When the Lord Takes Away

Monday, November 1, 2010.

Dottie's breathing grew slower as our three youngest children and I stood quietly beside her hospital bed. No one had to tell us what was about to happen to my wife and their mother. At 1:30 p.m. her battle with an as-yet-unidentified disease ended in peace. Pastor Miles Nelson, a friend who had waited with us, offered prayer before withdrawing to allow us some time at her bedside. We lingered there in silence. We knew these would be all-too-brief moments at her side. Yet these quiet minutes were soon over and I committed her to God's care with a tearful prayer of gratitude to the loving God who had sent Dorothy Dean into our lives.

We turned to face the confusing variety of unfamiliar responsibilities which now confronted us. We summoned the nurse to confirm her death before telephoning family and friends. Then came dealing with necessary forms for the hospital. We notified the funeral home and then stood a bed-side vigil until we could commit her silent form to the mortician's custody. For the first time in nearly a week we had no further reason to remain in the hospital. We sadly collected her things and ours, and soon were on our long and sad drive home. Less than twelve hours after Dottie's death, I retired to a bed I would never again share with her. Other family members were in the house, yet I could not have felt more alone if the whole world had abandoned me. I possessed no strength to battle the tears. I could scarcely muster ability to muffle the sound a bit. I was immersed in the first of what I have come to call my "grief attacks." I'm not sure how long this one lasted, but I know it ran its course. They always do.

Regaining some composure I found myself contemplating the nearly sixty years that God had given us together. How rare today for marriages to continue for that length of time. Heartbroken as I was, I knew I had been blessed. In that mid-night darkness the Lord first gave me the Scripture verse to which I returned again and again in my growing sorrow: "The Lord gave and the Lord has taken away; may the name of the Lord be praised" (Job 1:21 NIV).

Dwight, as my oldest son, read those words for me at her funeral. And they later appeared in many of my responses to the expressions of condolences we received. I did not blame God for Dottie's death although I knew it could not have happened without his permission. But I did thank him for giving us those years together. And I did see his hand in mercifully sparing her from the suffering and other trials she and I feared might lie ahead for her. Even more consequential, this word from the Scripture came to be the foundation of my life in the days that followed. Especially in my grief, I needed to remember how much the

Lord has blessed me, and to acknowledge that even with her death the Lord has not left me alone.

How wrong it would be to abandon my gratitude for what God had given me just because now I must deal with her absence from my life. Almost from our first meeting I have known that my wife's name Dorothy derives from a Greek word meaning "gift of God." I need to keep the goodness of God's gift foremost in my thinking, especially when her absence is dominating my life. I determined that this verse should become the pattern for my prayer life in the coming days. I recall how I began the prayer I offered when I first sat alone for a meal at my kitchen table: "I thank you, Lord, for every year you gave me with Dorothy, and I thank you for your continued presence in my life without her."

Since then I try to begin every one of my personal prayers with this petition. At first, things did not go smoothly. I choked up, struggled to get the words out, and wept. But I remembered, and I tried. Gradually, the words flowed more naturally almost like the Lord's Prayer in church services. Sometimes my voice still breaks; but the prayer's essence still lives within me. The past has been God's gift to me; and even when the heart of that gift is taken from me, he remains. I want to understand my suffering in this framework. The Lord gave and the Lord has taken away; may the name of the Lord be praised.

2. We Have Some Sad News

I was still in shock over Dorothy's death. Her hospitalization had been brief. Although I soon realized the end
was inevitable, its arrival and finality took my breath away.
A kind of numbness set in. But those of us at her bedside
soon recognized that we were the ones who had to share the
news with family and friends. We could not afford the lux-
ury of inactivity. My children and I huddled and divided
our list of phone calls to make. The confusion had begun.

I don't recall many of the details. I fear we may not
have made all the contacts we should have. Yet we started
the process of spreading the word. News got back to our retirement village a hundred miles west before we did. The
internet's social network reached almost everyone else.

During our meeting with the funeral director the next
morning, my daughter Bethany provided the information
for the obituary which later appeared in newspapers in
Pittsfield, Mass., and at Live Oak and Gainesville, Florida.
We still needed to share information and further details in
statements at the funeral itself, in contacts with those who
might not have heard, and in our responses to expressions
of sympathy. Words and actions conveyed condolences and

encouragement from near and far. Our retirement center officials and neighbors on our street. Friends and colleagues from the past. My former students.

The most complete statement took about three weeks to emerge after passing through several versions. By the end of November, this is the statement I was sending out:

Dorothy Pierce Dean
Sept. 2, 1927 - Nov. 1, 2010

On November 1, 2010 at 1:30 p. m. my dear wife, Dorothy May Pierce Dean, ended her earthly pilgrimage in Memorial Hospital at Jacksonville, Florida, in the eighty-fourth year of her life. Three of our children (Paul, Nathan and Bethany) and I were at her side. She died in full confidence that whether in life or in death, she was not her own but belonged to her faithful Savior Jesus Christ, who with his precious blood had fully satisfied for all her sins and redeemed her from all the power of the evil one.

This year her health had appeared good and she continued her usual schedule of activities until a short period of weakness in mid-October led to her hospitalization. Her final illness (apparently a form of leukemia) had appeared suddenly, and it claimed her quickly. She suffered consciously for only one of her five days in the hospital before the Lord mercifully gave sleep to the one we loved.

As sunset approached on November 4th we laid her to rest at Bixler Memorial Gardens East near our home at

Dowling Park, Florida. Her children and I confess that our
loss is almost greater than we can bear and that sadness
reaches into our souls. Yet we do not sorrow as those who
have no hope; we know that we shall see her anew when
our Lord Jesus returns to this earth.

Dottie was born in Porter, Maine on September 2, 1927
as fifth of the eight children of LeRoy Samuel Pierce and
his wife, Beatrice Sawyer. A graduate of Porter High
School (1945) and Berkshire Christian College (1951), she
later did specialized studies at North Adams (MA) State
College. In addition to serving at my side in pastorates in
Danville, P.Q., Canada; Springfield and Southfield, MA and
Pacific, MO, she was an important part of my ministry at
Berkshire Christian College and Gordon-Conwell Theological Seminary. Dorothy gave birth to our five children and
later taught in the Lenox, MA elementary schools for 15
years. After our retirement to Advent Christian Village in
Dowling Park, she taught with me in India, Japan, the Phil-
ippines and Mexico.

Our family has lost our closest friend, one whose love
and encouragement can never be fully recounted. Her husband, children (Dwight, David, Paul, Nathan, and Bethany), sisters (Marjory and Kay), brother (Dwight), 15
grandchildren, and 4 great grandchildren are saddened, but
not broken. We heartily thank God for sending this godly
woman to enrich our lives and draw us closer to Christ.
    The Lord has given, and the Lord has taken away.
Please join us in blessing the name of the Lord.
                    /signed/ David A. Dean

I lacked the emotional strength to speak at the funeral itself. So some form of this announcement is the first written expression of my grief. Preparing it served to intensify my awareness of how great my loss had been while reinforcing my gratitude for God's past gifts and for his continued presence even during these dark hours.

3. Seen in Her Face

Dorothy Dean's final stay in the hospital lasted five days. During the last three of them she seldom opened her eyes or spoke. Much of that time either our children or I stood or sat by her bedside unable to do much more than hold her hand, smooth back her hair, and assure her that I remained nearby.

When no one else was present, I searched her countenance for any sign that she knew I was there, or any evidence of a change in her condition. Except as her pain medication wore off, I detected no facial indication of what might be going on within her. What did impress me was how natural she looked. Her skin color was very much as it had been on those days before she first entered the hospital. Her single day of physical suffering had etched no wrinkles on her visage. Her facial muscles were not distorted by the experience. She lay there as in a peaceful slumber, appearing little different than when she had dozed in her lounge chair at home.

I commented to our children on her natural appearance. She looked as nice as when we attended church together or enjoyed a meal at a good restaurant. I knew she was seriously ill, but I could not tell it from her face. As Professor Higgins admits concerning Eliza Doolittle in "My Fair Lady," I had grown "accustomed to her face." Though we could no longer talk to each other, her appearance reassured me that I still had my wife with me. It encouraged me just to look at her.

Then something happened which altered my outlook in dramatic fashion. The transition may have come while I was taking comfort from her continuing to appear so natural and normal. And until the end that continued to be the case. While I did not detect any change in her appearance, at some point, I recognized what I had not seen before—the face of an old woman. I do not use the term in a derogatory way, but with the same tenderness and love I possessed before acknowledging its truth.

I never thought of Dorothy as old. I knew her chronological age. Yet she thought and acted like a person much younger. She loved people and activities and new experiences. "Let's go someplace," she often urged her workaholic husband. And as long as she lived she dressed brightly, attended parties, visited restaurants, and delivered birthday cards to shut-ins. I never thought of Dorothy as old.

When I perused her face she was still the same person who had been so active, but now I saw her advanced years. Closed lids now concealed the sparkle in her eyes. The smile had left her lips. Her readiness to jump into action and her interest in new experiences were now in her past.

Without these, she had become old. In a moment, without any change in her appearance, she was no longer vibrant and youthful but inactive and elderly. The truth forced itself upon me: I could not expect to have her at my side much longer.

Looking back, I suspect that deep within me the grief that in a few hours would crush my spirit was already dawning. I knew as well as anyone that old people die. I now realized that my wife was in that group. She was dying. So my acknowledging her as old actually became God's way of showing me that Dorothy Pierce and David Dean would soon complete their vows of lifelong faithfulness.

And, on November 1, 2010, it happened.

4. Is Black Colorful Enough?

Our children and I wanted to bury their mother in a bright and colorful dress.

Even after eighty-three birthdays she continued to prefer striking clothes. You could tell that from her pictures in our retirement center's most recent photo directories. Although the blue that matched her eyes was her favorite color (and mine, too), you might just as often find her wearing the lively yellow-green of spring or a bright pattern of multi-colored flowers. For our final portrait taken together a mere six weeks earlier, she had opted for a vibrant red blouse and a necklace in which quiet pastels both separated and highlighted the brilliant primary colors. Those hues expressed her personality, and that's why the girls in the family chose bright garments for her burial.

The funeral director appreciated the reasons for our preference and would gladly have complied with our wishes, except for one consideration. Her final illness had required several medical procedures which had visibly bruised her arms. Her clothes would require long sleeves. But not even our most extensive searches of her wardrobe at home could yield one dress with both the desired color and the needed arm length. At the time we could locate only a single garment capable of concealing the evidence of her final illness, and that dress was . . . black! Though we were certain she would have preferred to be dressed color- fully, we had no choice in the matter. Reluctantly, we took her black dress to the funeral home as our allotted time was running out.

In our grief we struggled against the haunting fear that we were failing her. Crimson, royal blue or even a bright yellow would have captured her bright outlook and still youthful spirit. How could a somber black convey those as- pects of her personality? Only those who have been in our place can imagine how badly we felt that we couldn't clothe her the way we knew she would have wished. We re- ally wanted to do better for her than black! Most of us were disappointed, some were close to being depressed. I think all of us felt guilty. Those feelings continued as I first ap- proached her sleeping form in the casket. The black dress gave no hint of enthusiasm or exuberance, though her gar- ment might have suggested her thoughtfulness and spiritual concerns. A colorful corsage in her hands (which Dave sug- gested) contrasted with the black garment on which it rested. That small splash of color may have jarred my memory of other things her dark clothing expressed.

God had been there in the midst of the disappointment when we felt we had no choice. He led us to the very same formal dress our children had given her for our golden wed- ding anniversary celebration nearly a decade ago. At the climax of that observance our entire family shared a de- lightful Caribbean cruise together. It was the gown she wore for our formal family portrait and for the reception when we met with the ship's captain. Since then she had worn it for more subdued dignity on an equally joyful occasion.

Yes, we were let down that we could not find something bright for our final gathering with her. Her gown in the casket was indeed black; yet, just as it had done ten years earlier, it bore faithful witness to the excitement and joy of our whole life together as a family. Black, yes. But worthy to represent the many blessings of the life she shared with us.

5. Caring for Dottie's Things

The funeral was over. My children and their families had departed. Completely alone for the first time, I felt surprise that I was doing as well as it seemed. No blanket of gloom smothered my days. My appetite was normal. I fell asleep quickly and enjoyed a full night's rest. Those things were (and continue to be) true.

However, I need to add some details concerning my claim about sleep. I kept busy during my waking hours, attacking my tasks with a vengeance. As I had done during my college years, I extended my days by rising earlier and retiring later than usual. For the first couple of months I ran on adrenalin and did not retire until exhaustion claimed me. I did sleep well, but my usual pattern would have included at least a couple more hours of rest.

I felt obligated to reduce the amount of the "stuff" around the house and to make what I kept more accessible. Neither Dottie nor I found it easy to throw things out. On occasions we had small successes when we would secretly discard an overused item belonging to the other. Last year we tried more than once to open boxes and make decisions about souvenirs, news clippings, and the like. But with our medical problems, the task proved just too daunting. Now her death has left me to go through these materials and decide what to keep, what to give to family members, and what to discard.

What could be simpler than that? Yet I found almost every item entangled with memories of our life together. Touching any one of them re-opened the fresh wounds from my sadness. Like holding again a receipt for living room furniture we bought before our wedding, or rereading our children's birth announcements. Though memories and tears were inescapable, I worked my way through sixty years of our life together. One box at a time. A few friends offered to help me, but this was something I had to take care of myself—even though blurred eyes kept me from seeing clearly. Around me an empty house. Within me a broken heart.

At the same time, I started to collect Dottie's clothing and to empty her bureau drawers and closet space. I recalled how she had looked in each dress as I folded and packed it with care. My daughter-in-law, Barbara helped me, but more work remained after she returned to her home. With most of Dorothy's clothing gone, regret seized me over failing to keep a certain blue and white dress. Both of us had considered it a favorite. She looked her best in blue. It matched her eyes. How could I have let it get away from me? It bothered me so much that later, when I found a bright yellow sun dress with white polka dots, I didn't let it out of my sight. It continues to brighten my closet. If I can't have Dottie, at least I'll hold on to that dress for a while. She would have wanted anything useful to be passed on to others, and that's what I have done—except for the yellow dress.

In a way, going through Dottie's keepsakes and souvenirs has been the hardest task I have faced. These items were more precious and personal to her than even her clothing and jewelry. I could look through each item into her heart. As I held them I almost felt as if she were back with me. And at the same time they made her more distant. Only by enumerating each article could I show how I met her in them all. But I can share their impact on me: they showed how much she loved the people in her life. More than any of her possessions, she treasured the people associated with them. Some items reinforced her many recent allusions to the security she had felt in her father's arms. Others pointed to her mother, brothers and sisters, husband, children, grandchildren, and even still unnamed expected babies. Among these "things" I re-discovered how very much she loved our children! With evidence scattered in many places, she may not have known how complete her collection for each of them was. Records of her weight while awaiting their arrivals. Birth announcements. Medical records through the years. Photos and portraits. Report cards and notes from teachers. Graduation invitations and programs. News clippings, Greeting cards they sent her. School and college yearbooks. Athletic honors. Wedding invitations with programs, napkins, and photos. Letters, photos and progress reports on all her children and grandchildren.

Only at the cost of being without her have I begun to comprehend how much she loved all of us. Gradually I have come to understand why she could not part with her "things." The obstacle had not been her love for objects (as I had mistakenly assumed), but her love for those associated with these items. Her "things" kept near to her those bound to her by love but separated by time and space and, in some cases, by death itself. I have witnessed eloquent testimony to how much she loved us—and could not bear to lose us. She loved her friends here in Florida; but she longed to be closer to her scattered children and family.

Well, I have sorted through most of her things now. Most of them are now gone from our home. But I am left with a richer understanding of how much we meant to her and with a better picture of how much we who are left have lost. In the process I've known the heartache of discarding some of the things she treasured and the joy of passing on to our children some tokens of their mother's love.

But I haven't parted with as much as I thought I would. Some things I've slipped into the Dean "Family History" file. And others are now in my boxes of "stuff." From now on I'll have a record of our first date, the exact time when we got engaged, and who was at our wedding. And before too long my children and others will be forced to sift through some of these same "things" again. May God grant that they may see in my possessions some evidence of how much I, too, have loved them.

6. My Urge to Talk

Apart from a few sermon illustrations, I have seldom informed anyone about what goes on within our family. That changed on the day Dorothy died.

Almost immediately I felt compelled to tell everyone about her death and share as much of the story as possible. Maybe the shock of her death had been so great I had felt compelled to tell the story over and over again to convince myself it had actually happened. Whatever the reason, my retelling the story soon turned into an unavoidable ritual.

It began with telephone calls we made to report the sad news to relatives and friends at a distance. I talked with people across the country. Because of the previous communications most were prepared for the news. But neither I nor my children (who made most of the calls) were able to stop there.

We felt compelled to share the full story. How she felt lethargic for a week. How her blood tests produced alarming reports. Her five days in the hospital. How her condition progressively deteriorated. About her coma. Then a description of her final moments.

By the time we arrived back home the story was well rehearsed. I remember that by then I had reduced each of her last five days to a single descriptive word. I repeated what happened to those who came to the visiting hours before the funeral. Later I volunteered the story to anyone who approached me to express condolences for the first time. Somehow I felt better after the experience by having done so.

At first, most people were interested and even volunteered questions if they suspected I left out something. Over time they showed less interest when they recognized familiar details. But I could almost always find people who hadn't heard and tell them. Or include the account in a letter I was composing.

This compulsion to tell and retell the story didn't surprise me. I had watched and listened to other grieving people as they did the same. Almost everybody does it for reasons that I am now better able to appreciate. At first I could hardly believe my wife's death had occurred. Though it at first seemed surreal, I found that repeating the story did reinforce its reality for me.

Telling the story served another purpose. It helped me to gain a better understanding of Dottie's last days. She and I had thought of her hospitalization as temporary, a time for

diagnosis and treatment. We anticipated she could soon return home to resume her ordinary activities.

Telling the story forced me to reconsider whether my
hope for this outcome had ever been warranted or whether
it had no basis. Without laboring details, I began to recognize that none of the hospital staff had ever promised us
more than that they might be able to begin treatment after
they identified her problem. (And by the time of her death a
firm diagnosis still eluded them.) In the meantime, their
procedures of renal dialysis and blood transfusions never
produced improvement that lasted for more than a few
minutes. Each retelling of the story helped me to accept
that Dottie's time had come. Her death had been the inevitable outcome of her medical condition.

It was not only that I needed to recount her story. There
were numerous other things on my mind, too. One day after
the funeral, I found a stack of incoming items in my mail-
box. From their size and texture, I surmised they must be
sympathy cards. I counted thirty of them. "Wow! I must
tell, Dottie;" I said to myself, "She'll never believe we got
so many." The words proved enough to call the tears.

I could never tell her—not today, not tomorrow, not
ever in this life. Thirty envelopes may not be a big deal, but
being unable to tell my lifelong helpmate about them is!
Arguably this has been the greatest heartache in all my sorrow. I can no longer share the little joys of my life with my
dearest friend. Deceptively, it sounds like such a small
thing; but you can't convince me of that.

Some time ago, we had a beautiful flannel blanket on one edge of which a section of binding had come loose. Dorothy put it away so she could re-attach it when she was sewing. But we never could relocate it. One day after the funeral I knelt down in a closet to open a shopping bag. Folded up near its top, the missing blanket. The two year mystery solved! I was thrilled. I jumped to my feet, the blanket in my hand and called out, "Dottie, Look at what I found!" Before the words were airborne, I knew I could not share the news with her. I needed to tell her, but she was not here to listen. I have had no heavier heartache in all of my sorrow. I can no longer share the little joys of life with my closest companion. It may sound like such a small thing. But it doesn't feel that way. My heart protests. It isn't fair that I can no longer share these special moments with her.

Not a day goes by without something happening that I would routinely have mentioned to her. A young wife in our neighborhood has reached her weight loss goal. Sebastian—her newest great-grandson—has been born in Oregon. We had a large crowd at church today. These things would have made her happy. Yet I can't tell her.

I don't consider myself to be a "talker," but you do have to talk in order to share the little things of life. Passing the report on is what makes those insignificant matters important. Though what one says may not technically be a secret, the act of sharing it with someone you love gives a

special quality to your relationship. That's what I most miss
when I have something I need to say.

Strange, isn't it that the same grief that loosens my
tongue about some matters also ties my tongue over other
things I desperately want to say? I suspect this problem will
not soon go away.

Part Two

Looking Back: Months Two, Three, Four

The continuing shock of Dottie's death moderated my pain during the Thanksgiving and Christmas season. It enabled me to face the initial confusion until the frantic pace of life slowed. I scarcely completed the most urgent tasks before my energy level collapsed. The awful finality of her absence began to dawn on me. These factors combined to force me to review the preceding year.

That time period had brought each of us several medical problems. Mine appeared more serious, but we felt her health improved remarkably. Though we both knew we were aging, it seemed like a good year for her. I never guessed it would be her last.

My most intense sorrow still lay ahead, but my mind was clearing as I turned to contemplate the recent past. I began to wonder how the preceding months were related to the day she died. Exploring that query I came to see God's gracious hand in all that had taken place.

During these months I braced myself to face two family holidays without her. At the same time I looked back to discover the value of our conversations, visits, and other activities as God-given preparations for the future.

7. Final Conversations

During those early weeks without Dorothy, I began to
see dimly the outline of God's gracious hand during the
previous months. The Lord had been merciful by providing
us the opportunity to talk to each other about death for one
of us and life afterwards for the survivor.

Dottie and I had earlier discussed these matters, especially in recent years as sickness invaded our home more
frequently. We had wondered aloud about which one of us
would die first. She often said she didn't want to leave me.
The feeling was mutual, but I would warn her that in our
society husbands usually die first. We had each outlived our
parents and knew our days together were growing shorter.
We had made our decisions on Health Care Proxies, Do Not
Resuscitate orders, and our final wishes about "heroic" in-
terventions. We discussed funeral plans and burial sites.

However, during the past year our Heavenly Father lovingly forced us to explore these matters in greater detail.
The urgency lay in my heart problems. It grew as my hospitalizations—some including risky procedures—became

more frequent. We pledged to take care of one another as long as we were able and agreed that God would certainly do so after one of us died. And we talked about what either one of us should do in the event we lost the other. We gathered the documents we would need: birth and marriage certificates, insurance papers, bank and other financial records, wills, deeds, names to contact, and the like. Because of those conversations, most of them were in one file drawer when I needed them. The Lord even broadened the discussion of our "end of life issues" to include family relations, financial matters, housing plans, and our own love for one another. We explored our feelings about death. Neither of us was afraid to die. Each wanted to live to care for the other. "I don't want to leave you;" she said with tears, "but I'm sure you could care for yourself more easily without me than I could without you." In my heart I knew she was right. God spared her the limitations she feared.

I can see now how kind it was of God to provide this precious opportunity to say good bye to each other. Later would have been too late for she was unconscious before either of us grasped the seriousness of her illness. When I did know, it was too late.

"I am afraid one of us will die," I had told her more than once "before I will be able to tell you how much you mean to me." But in our last year together the Lord extended us the priceless privilege of expressing our love to each other, of apologizing to one another for our failures, and of thanking each other for our life together. Inadequate

though my words may have been to express myself well,
God did give us both the opportunity. Many never experience this grace.

Neither of us sensed it at the time, but I now see that
our loving Heavenly Father was preparing us for the unexpected arrival of the enemy Death.

8. "Mean Season" (1) – Thanksgiving

Less than a month into my grief, a publication from Hospice warned about difficulties I might encounter during the coming holidays. It offered helpful suggestions about how to prepare for the stress. I knew I didn't have long to wait for the arrival of what the young widow, Lisa Beamer, calls the "mean season" of Thanksgiving and Christmas.

Dottie helped to make the preparations for Thanksgiving 2010 before she became ill. Our three southern children and their families would entertain all the Deans who could come to Camp Dixie, near Fayetteville, NC. Nestled in a small valley, its facilities offered a comfortable motel with a nearby kitchen and dining room overlooking a delightful pond. After her death we decided to go ahead with the plans anyway.

For me it would be about a nine hour drive, but I never hesitated about making the trip—even alone. My wife and I had never done much talking while traveling by car. After she gave up driving, she would often fall sleep while we

rode; so the silence was not overwhelming as I drove north-
ward alone. Whenever I sensed the reality that she wasn't
with me and that she would never again ride at my side, another grief attack would strike. It would mix my inner emptiness with self-pity. I felt that half of me were gone. My
sorrow seemed almost unbearable. But these dark times
didn't last as long as I had feared they might.

I was among the first to arrive, accompanied by my son,
Nathan. I met him at his home in Augusta, Georgia and he
drove the rest of the way. Once there I put on my best face
for all who came. Even so, several grief attacks did surface—generally when I was in my room alone. Our family's schedule probably allowed me too much time by myself. Without Dorothy among those present, it crushed me
that I could not phone her with news of my safe arrival, or
report to her who was there, or describe the happenings at
Thanksgiving dinner. Our numbers increased daily until
we had fourteen for turkey at our afternoon dinner table.
We sat down almost three weeks to the hour from the time
of Dottie's grave-side service.

The children and I were able to talk about their mother,
yet with my emotions so close to the surface I limited most
of my comments to phrases. I looked around the dinner table longing to see her face while someone commented how
difficult she would have found it to let the younger wives
do all the cooking. We concluded our meal leisurely with
conversation over pie. Everyone was aware who was missing from our meal.

Most of us remained together until Saturday morning. Yet, too quickly our gathering was over, and I would soon be on my way home. When we lined up our cars, I became the first to leave, and at 9:15 a. m. our family Thanksgiving gathering was over.

I drove off in my otherwise empty Buick with a wave and a smile to all. How good it was to share Thanksgiving with so many of my family. I would not have missed it for the world. But the painful awareness of Dottie's absence depressed the mood as I drove home. I should have realized that my grief would become worse before it got easier.

9. For One Last Time

My son Dave and most of his family left home as soon as possible after learning of his mother's death. He had taken a week to be with us earlier in the year, but wasn't able to see her during her final illness. When Dave did arrive he told me how grateful he was that he and his wife had spent that time with us last spring. They had not been alone. By my count, all our five children, five of our fifteen grandchildren, and two great grandchildren had been in our home during the last year.

At one point, David stunned me by commenting, "You know, all of us thought we were coming down to see you one last time." That the purpose of their trips might be to have a final visit with me had never crossed my mind. I do remember wondering in Dave's case about the timing. He arrived on relatively short notice and at an inconvenient season for him. But I hadn't given it much thought. I had other things on my mind. In late 2009, a temporary disability from a stroke had sent me to the hospital. Soon after, it took a surgical biopsy to confirm I was cancer free. Then heart rhythm problems, new medications, a pacemaker implant, eventually a cardio-version and an atrial flutter ablation. That's five hospitalizations and three trips to the operating room in less than a year. I took them in stride, but the heart problem remained. And I can understand why my children might have wanted to see me while they still could. Yet these visits implied something more than my children's motivation. They also opened up a window into my wife's heart. My illnesses required each of us to face the reality of death. To prepare for life without a spouse. And to say our goodbyes. She expected I would likely go first. She must have shared her heart with our children. I began to realize she had been more concerned about me than she admitted. The idea for them to come soon and to see me "for one last time" must have been hers. She did not want her children and their father to miss a final visit with each other.

Now as I reflect, I wonder if these visits do not also reveal something about God's heart. Why should I have had poor health the year before Dorothy's death and relatively good health since then?

Was not the Lord using my illnesses to draw our children back home for one final visit with their mother? Their time with her could be relaxed and stress-free because it was not her but me they were worried about. She could hear from their own lips the expressions of their love, their promises to come at her call, and their assurance they would take care of her if she should be left alone. Their time together could produce the warmth of family closeness because their focus of concern was on me rather than on themselves. As a bonus Dottie and I could share their visits together. And God was arranging it for both of us.

Grief can be a great eye-opener. The tears it places in our eyes may also bring greater clarity to our vision. What I could not see during the final year of our life together I can now see in our first year apart. God was preparing our family for the impending time of separation by bringing us together in the months before her death. My illnesses opened the door to an end of life intimacy for the two of us. A culminating fulfillment of our wedding promises to each other. They also gave our children the precious, even if unanticipated, chance to really be with their mother "for one last time."

Years ago Dottie's mother, on the evening before her death, informed her doctor about the wonderful day God had given her. She had been free of pain and all her eight children had visited with her. Dorothy often expressed her hope the Lord might bless her the same way. Nearly thirty years later, God treated my wife even better. He gave her a whole year of fairly good health and extended relaxed visits with each of her children. Grief now brings tears to my eyes, but I cannot let it blind me to God's gracious gifts to Dorothy during our final year together.

10. Mean Season (2) – Christmas

As Christmas approached I opted to stay "home for the holidays." I knew any of the children would have welcomed me; but sooner or later I would have to spend Christmas alone. I chose to do it now.

Broken hearted that I could not give Dottie a Christmas present this time, I bravely wrapped and mailed the gifts that she and I had purchased during the year for various family members. I sent off a mere handful of Christmas cards since I was still working my way through a mountain of "thank you notes." I put up our small lighted Christmas tree on the porch plus the crèche and Christmas banner on my front lawn. And I made my reservation for the festive Christmas dinner at our retirement center. But as Christmas neared I worried whether planning to stay home had been the right decision.

Acting on a Hospice recommendation, I chose to replace some traditional activities that might stir up too painful memories. So I chose to by-pass the Christmas Eve service at church for a quiet meal at a friend's home. Then I decided to open my gifts on Christmas evening rather than in the morning. These changes would alter the pattern that Dottie and I had followed.

I thought I was fully prepared until the chilling question struck me, "How will you get through Christmas morning?" This had always constituted "the holiday" for our family. Opening Christmas stockings. Relaxing over a special breakfast. Distributing gifts from the tree. These all led up to a big dinner. Yet the changes I contemplated left nothing at all for me to do on Christmas morning. I could already feel the crushing loneliness of waking on Christmas day to an empty house.

Then I recalled the advice I had given others in their sorrow: try to make Christmas morning happier for someone else. Why not volunteer to help serve breakfast at the assisted living facility in our retirement center? Looking back, this activity made my day! I had no time to feel sorry for myself when I jumped out of bed on Christmas morning. I was still adjusting my red Santa hat as I drove over to Dacier Manor. Soon I was starting the coffee and wishing "Merry Christmas" to a group of my long-time friends. We were all separated from family on Christmas. Following the meal, several of us stayed to talk and share memories. There is nothing like good conversation to shame tears into staying away.

The noon banquet in the main dining room with hundreds of other friends proved equally delightful. Laughter and festivities joined the traditional menu in driving grief away, even providing me a convincing excuse for an afternoon nap. And without any depressing overtones.

No grief attack approached me until later in the day. It was evening and I was driving alone to a second Christmas dinner in a nearby town. Darkness was settling in—which is often a depressing time for me. For some reason my mind turned to the India of a decade past where Dottie and I spent six months. At Christmas time we felt unbearably isolated from our home, country and family. But at least we had each other! This year I did not even have her. Sadness and loneliness forced their way into my spirit. I slowed down and wiped my eyes enough to restore my vision of the road, and to remind myself that God had given her to me for almost sixty years. I must not allow two months without her to blot out that wonderful blessing.

I'll never doubt God was convicting me of my self-pity and reassuring me of his continued presence. The Lord's nearness saved my Christmas and continued with me after I returned home. There he and I, just the two of us, opened my gifts to crown a serious but enjoyable day.

Did I miss my wife on this special day? You better believe I did! So much that I did not dare to compare today's joy with the good times she and I enjoyed in Christmases past. Those holidays with her were precious, but I did not yet have the strength and courage to dust off the memories and look at them too closely. Still, they are great memories and their time will come.

11. Final Preparations

Looking back over Dottie's final year, I realize that I should have noticed her failing health. She spent more time in her living room recliner and showed less interest in things which were once important to her. She had gradually given up knitting, crocheting, sewing and her other crafts. Like her mother before her, Dottie loved books and cherished her collection of a complete set of Grace Livingston Hill's writings. She had loved them since childhood and often revisited one or another novel. Slowly she turned away from them entirely and also from her favorite historical and Christian novels. She reduced her daily reading to the King James Bible of her childhood. And sometimes she would replace reading with listening to the Bible on an audio tape, followed by working silently through her prayer list.

Her books of memory-strengthening Sudoku puzzles took up less of her time and television (interspersed with naps) took over more. If letters required replies, I inherited the privilege of composing them. She continued writing and recording checks in her bank account, but asked me to take over sending out family birthday and anniversary cards. In the process I became familiar with where she kept her records and materials. I helped her to organize and update her files.

Housework became a bigger chore for her, giving me a chance to brush up on my skills of bed making, dusting, running a vacuum cleaner, and returning household items to their proper places. The washer and dryer were about the only equipment I didn't learn how to use. (But I have since.)

Most significantly, preparing meals interested her less and less. At first we compensated by increasing the frequency of eating out. However, it soon became clear that I needed to assist in meal preparation at home. I expanded my boyhood skills of boiling water and toasting bread to include the art of scrambling eggs. Yet I still needed to step it up a notch.

I started by helping her, advanced to accepting directions. Finally I started to plan meals and she offered her aid in preparing them. Soon I got carried away, even attempting fish chowder on one occasion and stew beef gravy on another. Dottie even pronounced the chowder as good. In the process I investigated her recipe file and identified her favorite cook books and most often used recipes. You would almost have thought she was teaching me how to cook. No matter; I was learning.

Over the years my wife had been the self-confident and gifted administrator in our home. She kept our activity

schedule, posted appointments on the calendar, and alerted
me to their approach. Last year the task became more de-
manding as the number of our medical appointments increased. We recorded and planned for them together. But as
their pace picked up, she became less sure of herself, hesitated at making decisions and trusted less in her memory.
With good reason.

In the background our medical escapades kept us in
emotional uncertainty. Her own treatments provided encouraging results, but these were offset in my case by on-
going problems which emphasized an uncertain future. She
began to look to me for leadership in family matters she
had always enjoyed caring for herself. Gradually I became
administrator of the entire household: ordering, shopping,
scheduling, accompanying her to see the doctor, paying
bills, returning phone calls. This provided Dottie a sense of
greater security, and I came to learn the inside operations of
the household.

In November, after her death, I began to discern what I
had not seen earlier. God had begun to prepare me for the
time when I would be forced to live my life, carry on my
ministry, and keep house without her. And so I go about
these household tasks with a heavy heart, yet with a much
greater appreciation for all Dorothy has done for me over
the years. I miss her so much and long to have back the former days with her. Yet—even with her absence—I know
the God who guided her to prepare me for the present is the
same One who promised "I will never leave you nor forsake you" (Heb 13:5).

12. Memorial Flowers

Spring rushed into northern Florida with exuberance this year. After enduring what seemed like weeks of cold, cloudy, raw, windy weather, we residents were at an eye's blink bathed in the warmth of sunshine and engulfed by the glory of flowering trees and shrubbery. Around my house it's the azalea bushes that capture your attention.

At my back deck a few days ago the azalea blossoms reached out to me by the hundreds in breath-taking brilliance. Several years back I trimmed these bushes severely and they have retaliated by sharing few flowers with us since then. Dottie loved those blossoms and missed them very much—especially last year. But now they are back filling, almost every empty place on the now symmetrical shrubbery with large, well-formed blooms and a spectacular display of color. I'm never sure how to describe them. A few are peach colored, but the majority are two-toned cherry, or is it fuchsia? At any rate, Dottie would have been thrilled to see this year's display.

Gazing out on them I found myself saying aloud, "These are Dottie's memorial flowers." And so they are.

When I drove her to the hospital last October, the winter
she would never see was nowhere near. Now the cold
weather has passed and the spring—which she is not going
to see, either—is underway. And God has painted this
breathtaking floral masterpiece for me in remembrance of
her.

And so I have watched these azaleas with special interest. I've observed their increase in number, in size, and in
beauty. I have enjoyed them for her as I now do so many
things for her, painfully aware that she is not here to do
them herself. Like the Christmas gifts she had picked out,
but did not live to send. Like birthday cards for the great
grandchildren whose arrival she had expected to live long
enough to see.

One day I sensed I was losing those memorial flowers.
Their glory was silently slipping away. Petals began to fade
and shrivel, and the raindrops and breeze came to deposit
them gently on the ground. As the prophet well understood,
"The grass withers and the flowers fall" (Isaiah 40:7).
Slowly at first, but then more rapidly as the days grow
longer. Now so few remain, clinging feebly to the branches,
with subdued color and missing petals.

Dottie's memorial flowers, or not, I cannot keep them.
No more than I could keep her when her days were full and
her strength was failing. Still, the Lord has been so good to
me. When he gave her to me in my youth, color and excitement entered my life. Now he has sent these flowers to help

me remember her at a time when so much of that earlier color has faded out.

I've savored these flowers, and now I wait for the Lord to send me Dottie's memorial flowers again next year. I'm confident He understands how much I need enjoyable things to look forward to.

Part Three

My Darkest Hours: Months Five, Six, Seven

During my first three or four months without Dorothy, I was too sad, too confused, and too busy to undertake any amount of serious writing. I have since written about those days; but I could not do so then. Yet my thinking continued to clear towards the end of this period. I began to discern how God had been preparing us for our separation.

Until then my sorrow had been both real and painful, even though I had been spared its full force. My initial shock from Dottie's death had subsided enough that grief's full force could sweep over me. This ushered in the three months of my greatest suffering. My emotions stirred deeper in my heart and at the same time rose closer to the surface. They were eager to disrupt my daily life. A deep sadness increased within me, and I thought more often about Dorothy. I grieved over her. She remained the object of my sorrow. And yet I suspect that the real focus of my attention was on me and my pain at being deprived of her companionship.

At the same time that my sorrows multiplied and intensified, I was also recovering my ability to think about their nature and meaning. With my grief attacks alternating with times of quiet contemplation I began to commit to paper some of those experiences which stirred me most deeply.

13. Even "Meaner" Holidays

NEW YEAR'S DAY. The new year began even easier
than had Christmas. I launched it by attending an old-time
Watch Night Service at the local Baptist Church. Dottie and
I had welcomed in 2010 with that same group a year ago.
Though I arrived by myself and felt very much alone this
time, I had the opportunity to share with the congregation
how the Lord had been my comfort during the past two
months. Surprise: no grief attacks during the ninety minutes
there! Still I didn't linger long after the new year arrived
and the service ended. Frankly, I feared I might break down
in personal conversations. Besides I was scheduled to serve
coffee for breakfast at the Dacier Manor assisted living res-
idence. I needed some sleep.

Driving home reminded me that welcoming the new
year had been more important to me than to Dorothy. I always stayed up to greet the new year, while she kept to her
usual bedtime. So being alone at midnight this year was not
much different from when I was married. It would be the
daylight hours of January 1st that brought the surprises.

They didn't come at the assisted living facility where a leisurely interval for conversation followed breakfast. All was routine and, with a promise to see them at lunchtime, I left shortly for another appointment.

Between serving at those two meals, I attended a brunch with several friends in one of the Village's smaller neighborhoods. Here I met a new aspect of grief for the first time. I wasn't aware of it as we mixed and paired off for conversation. Although no one intended my discomfort, I suddenly realized that I didn't fit. In a group of seven people, I was the only one not married to another person in that room. For nearly sixty years I had been a married man in a world of married couples. Now I was the "odd" person, the only one not part of a couple. I had no one to talk to unless I displaced someone else in a conversation. What should I do? Keep quiet and appear unfriendly? Push my way into others' conversations? I wasn't sure what to do. More problematic, I was uncertain about who I had become.

Since I was no longer married, who was I now? I would have given anything to have had Dorothy back at my side. Then I would at least have known who I was and how to act. Suddenly my identity became one of the most mystifying aspects in my grief. At the brunch friends who only wanted to make my life easier probably never guessed how perplexed I was. They could not know how desperately I needed to understand my new role as a widower—a suddenly single man. Later I learned of Elizabeth Elliot's feeling that when she joined other missionaries after Jim's death, she was a "misfit," a "fifth wheel (who threw) things off balance by just being there." Her friends tried to help but they could not do anything about the fact that she was no longer "half a couple." Now it's I who must self-consciously discover how I fit into a group and how I should act towards others. I may have learned that I am only half of my old self.

Now I must discover who is the half that still remains. I was unprepared for this confusion over my new identity. It is an unanticipated ingredient of my grief. Words fail my attempts to explain my new disorientation and my awkwardness in its grip. I met it first at a New Year's Day brunch, and it has hung around ever since.

VALENTINE'S DAY. If, before this year, you asked me to evaluate Valentine's Day I would have assured you it is a lesser holiday. It isn't that Dottie didn't like candy, or cards, or flowers. Except maybe for the early years of our marriage, she and I just didn't pay much attention to the day. So I was unprepared for that January morning when I went grocery shopping at the nearest Wal-Mart and encountered the first display of Valentine merchandise. One glance and I fell apart. I could not escape the haunting feeling that I couldn't get my wife anything for Valentine's Day. The same emotion had overpowered me in the days before Christmas. It made sense then because we always exchanged gifts at Christmas. But seldom on Valentine's Day! Why should every heart-laden display steal my composure and send me in search of a quieter aisle where other customers wouldn't notice how upset I was?

The question walked out of the store with me. Why should I feel as I had? Since it was not because of my inability to continue a practice, maybe it was regret that I had never formed the Valentine Day habit in the first place. I wonder if those displays did not serve as symbols to convict me of my thoughtlessness. I had failed to express my affection for Dorothy in the simple and romantic ways that would have lightened her steps. This was the problem. Not Valentine gifts I could not give; but rather the gifts I did not give when I could have done so. It was now too late to express my love for her in the outward ways she probably longed for.

And this is where grief cuts the deepest. I reproach myself that I have never been very expressive, and have seldom unveiled my deepest feelings. Dorothy's death has revived my memories of a string of ways in which I must have disappointed her. Wall pictures I never hung. Places I never took her. Desired items I told her we could not afford. Trees I never cut down, and bushes I never planted. Greeting cards I neglected to send. I console myself that I did the really important things, and granted many of her incidental requests. And I reassure myself that it may have been my lack of emotional outbursts that drew her to me in the first place.

Yet, I cannot escape grief when it points out my guilt. I know too well my failures. I did let her down, and I can't do anything now about it. Only the assurance of Scripture can bring me relief: "This is how we set our hearts at rest in his presence whenever our hearts condemn us. For God is greater than our hearts, and he knows everything" (1 John 3:19-20, NIV). The same God who knows how clumsily and ineptly and infrequently I showed my wife how much I loved her also knows my love was real. He who loves me forgives my failures, offers me his grace, and invites me to forgive myself.

My daughter also loves me. On a Valentine's card she sent me this year, she added this encouragement:

> *"Dear Daddy, I just wanted to remember you on Valentine's Day! Mom loved you so very much and I just needed to remind you of that on this holiday. Our talks each day help to fill the hole in my heart left when she died. I love you! Thank you for being such a godly father and husband."* Like her mother, she has an amazing sensitivity to my needs. And a great sense of timing!

I still wonder why these two lesser holidays have been so much harder than memory-loaded ones like Thanksgiving and Christmas. Might it be that the initial shock of Dorothy's death with its dulling of sorrow's pain had begun to wear off after a couple of months? Or had the passage of time brought me through those early days of emotional confusion over legal and business tasks into a more relaxed period when I could start thinking about my former life and my future directions? All I can say for certain is that I was finding the early months of 2011 to be harder rather than easier.

14. Empty Place in My Bed

My working day was about to start. As I had done so many times before, I reached out cautiously through the darkness to discover whether Dottie was still there beside me. Of course, she wasn't. She hasn't been there for four months now. Quickly loneliness rushed in, and it seemed as though Lord Tennyson had me in mind when he described the "tears of a widower when he moves his doubtful arms and feels her place is empty."

Shame at my instinctive reflex quickly joined my sadness. I have adjusted to the empty space beside me and should not have expected her to be here. I even sleep on different sides of the bed on alternate nights to de-emphasize how things used to be. And I think this is the first time I have been caught off guard in this way. Yet that's where loneliness is for me now. I'm not usually aware it's still around, though it's never far away. It has retreated into the quietness. It waits for me in the night hours. It seeks to control the twilight between consciousness and sleep. This morning it succeeded!

Still, don't think loneliness is in control. God graciously keeps my "aloneness" at a reasonable distance, allowing a return of my joys of home, family and daily life. I feel good about returning to the house from outside activities. I can find a quiet sense of accomplishment in meals I prepare, and even sometimes actually like my own cooking. Each sunset brings me a sense of satisfaction that God continues to keep his promise never to leave me. And each new dawn reveals the gift of another opportunity to be of some use to God's kingdom. Not only that. When loneliness does pounce on me, God brings back images and feelings from almost sixty years of marriage. I want to keep alive those memories of how much and for how long God has blessed me. While loneliness may use the empty place in my bed to reduce me to tears, God overrules it to remind me (and to renew the joy) of precious moments given to us on those rare occasions when we shared sleepless nights together. Today, our six months in South India a dozen years ago came back to my mind. We lived so close to the equator that the hours of darkness just about equaled those of daytime. Each evening about 6:00 twilight took over, and a chronic shortage of electricity denied us enough power even to illuminate our fluorescent "tubes." We sat around as long as we could in the darkness and then retired early out of boredom. Almost every night we were wide awake long before dawn.

This otherwise useless time provided us a chance to talk with one another. Our whispered conversations gave opportunity for the small talk which life's fast pace often crowds out. We lay there in the darkness with only thin mattress pads separating us from steel bed platforms. We chatted about our past, the previous day's activities, our disappointments, our plans, and anything else that came to mind. Those times of sharing brought us as close to one another as we have ever been.

How thoughtful of God to use the empty space in bed beside me to grant me a new experience of the priceless closeness he had given us to share a decade ago. And this the Lord has promised to renew again for us in the future. And through my tears I smile because I can almost hear Scripture taunt the enemy, "O Death, where is your sting?" (1 Cor 15:55 ESV).

15. Holding Her Hand

I was sitting beside them because Bob saw me looking for a seat and invited me to join him and Cathy. So there I was just a few rows from the front listening as my former colleague, Dr. Haddon Robinson was winding up one of his masterful sermons. Just then I caught a glimpse of Bob and Cathy's clasped hands.

Before realizing what was happening, tears gathered just below the surface. That's how my little grief attacks sneak up on me. Out of nowhere. Suddenly. Unexpectedly. No warning. There in a pair of clasped hands a silent reminder of Dottie's hand. The one I had often held, but would never do again in this life. I felt my shoulders begin to tremble on the edge of deeper emotions. The internal struggle to regain control of myself began. I mustn't let anyone suspect that my grief still lingers, even after the five months that have been so long for me and have raced by for others. Once I would have been embarrassed if I saw a grown man cry in public. Now I was that grown man.

Yet grief still lurks on the edges of my emotions. I miss
her very much, even after I've made many adjustments to
produce what my daughter Bethany calls "the new normal."
Daily life has become bearable once again. I joke, laugh at
things which may not really be funny, enjoy my favorite
food, take in a party. But I've just been reminded that I cannot hold Dottie's hand any more, and that merits a good
cry.

We had held hands more in later years. Like many our
age, Dottie had one gimpy knee that gave her trouble. The
pain would have been bad enough, but at crucial moments
she couldn't rely upon it to support her. Unsteady when she
stood and off balance when she walked, she came to rely on
a cane (or even a walker when I wasn't with her). But most
of the time while walking we just held hands. Even an article ten years ago in *Village Life* observed that "the Deans,
when out and about in the Village, invariably hold hands."
She found security in the unity of our hands. Clasping
hands kept us close to each other. It felt right, and confirmed our life-long commitment to take care of one another. Now, we can't do it anymore.

We first held hands as sophomores in college, awk-
wardly and tentatively, in February of 1949. We were on
our initial date to a church Valentine party in Melrose High-
lands, a suburb of Boston. We would continue the practice
for 61 years. Now, we can't do it anymore.

We held each other's hands in the little Advent Christian church at Kezar Falls, Maine, on Saturday, June 2,

1951. Fresh from our college graduation, we confessed our love and exchanged our rings and committed ourselves to one another alongside another couple in a double wedding ceremony. Our college president, Rev. Carlyle B. Roberts, asked us to join hands as he prayed God's blessing on our union. Now we can't join our hands anymore.

So also at other memorable times in our life together. In November, 1952 at Asbestos, Quebec, Canada, when I stood helplessly by and held her hand as the birth of our firstborn son drew near. Later in Pittsfield, Massachusetts, with her life in the balance, we held hands as I asked God to spare her life from the spreading poison of a ruptured appendix. She repaid the favor in August, 1984 at Rockland, Maine, holding my hand and interceding for my recovery from a heart attack. Who can tell at how many other times and places we joined hands? Now we can do it no more.

"I love your hands," Dottie would say to me in recent years as she looked at them and stroked them with hers. No explanation, but I could sense she meant what she said. I'm sure she saw a person's hands as the main instrument for transforming love from a sweet sentiment into loving action. At least I can see that in "Her Father's Hands," a free verse poem with which she remembered her dad a decade and a half after his death. What lingered in her memory? "Strong hands work[ing] to provide for a family of ten." Loving hands" carrying her to bed after her tonsils were removed . . . . "Gentle hands" placing a new baby sister into her arms when Dottie was ten. " Protective hands" which reassured her after a hunter's stray bullet came too close.

"Friendly hands ... welcom[ing] each new son- and daughter-in-law into the family.". . . "Trembling hands" clutching hers as they parted after his first heart attack. The hands of this hard-working, no-nonsense, Yankee mill worker had given Dottie a glimpse into his heart. She loved her father's hands long before she loved mine. And she well remembered her last lingering look at them: "His hands were still, and still beautiful, as they lay crossed at his waist—forever still." She felt the finality then as I do now. I can hold her hand no more.

My last memory, though, is not of a casket, but of a hospital bed where I took her hand in response to her plaintive plea, "David, help me." I could hold her hand in mine; but I could not ease her pain any more than could her deceased mother, to whom she also called in her closing minutes of consciousness.

Now I can hold her hand no more. Yet this harsh fact bids me recall the joys of the life and love we shared— fresh and vibrant in youth, tested in the fire of life's trials, withstanding even the face of death itself, and clinging to a loving God who will never leave us nor abandon us.

If I can only struggle through the tears, maybe I can reenter the joy of those memories— and even know once again how nice it was to hold her hand.

16. My Smile, Her Tears

The thought of my daughter, Bethany, and her family coming to spend Easter with me was uppermost in my mind. She would be the first of my children to come to Florida since some of us were together for Thanksgiving. She arrived about 11:30 p. m. on Good Friday and rushed into the house to greet me as the rest of her family unloaded the car. I was thrilled to see her and was enjoying the moment. Then I noticed that she was weeping. Without thinking I asked her, "What is it?" She composed herself long enough to reply, "This is the first time I have come back just to see my father." This was her first homecoming without her mother to embrace her. Suddenly my joy dissipated and I was broken-hearted for her.

Beyond that, I was stunned that my grief could make me so insensitive to Bethany's sorrow. Since we both mourned over the same loss I had assumed we would feel the same way when we saw each other. For almost six months now I have lived alone in this house, and have adjusted to the absence of her mother. The numbing sense of deprivation has subsided, though I still experience lonely times. I am accustomed to empty rooms and to isolating silence. I now know as I come up the ramp to my kitchen door that Dottie's smiling face and welcoming voice will not greet me. But this is Bethany's first return to a home in which her mother has always before awaited her with joy.

I wonder how could I have been so unprepared for her pain? My daughter's most sympathetic supporter had been caught up too much in his own excitement at seeing her. Having her home to fill my emptiness made me insensitive to how overwhelming her loneliness would become. Seeing only me highlighted the absence of her mother and the loss of their special bond.

Ironically, the grief which should have brought us together in the opening moments of our visit served instead to accentuate the differences in the way we felt its pain. Our shared sorrow served rather to push us apart. The same experience of seeing one another warmed my heart and broke hers. I should have expected her sorrow to express itself differently than mine.

"Your mother belonged as much to you as she did to me," 1 had told the children as we parted after Dottie's burial. And she really did. Yet with a significant difference. Though some of the details might be vague, I still remember the two decades of my life before I had even met their mother. But they have no memories of a time when she was not in their lives. In turn she had carried each of them within her own body, suffered with them through their birth experiences, and served as a comforting presence during their childhood. They lost more than their closest friend. They lost the one who brought them into this world. I too remember my own mother's death and the awful pain of being severed from my past. As Bethany's father I wish I had been more sensitive to my only daughter's great loss. However, the first few moments of a visit do not a weekend make. Awkward though it may have been, that initial encounter provided a helpful reminder that each of us must experience sorrow in our own way, from our own perspective, through our own personality, and according to our own time schedule. In grief, one size does not fit all. Sooner or later everyone will have to walk through the same dark valley. Yet when passing through shadows which conceal unknown and unwelcome trials, we will find ourselves on private and personal paths.

Bethany and I have walked into the same dark valley on this visit, yet on our personal paths. We exchanged differing versions of the same memories. We examined some of her mother's possessions to share our thinking on what she would have wanted done with them. We contemplated what Dottie meant to others in our family and how that compares to her place in our hearts. We conjectured about how the loss we have experienced will play out in the future. All of these things we did not in formal sessions but in a casual sharing of our recent difficult experiences. And I hope she may have detected in my joy at having her come home a promise that her own tears will yet give way to a mounting joy at being with others who love her.

We may have begun this visit on the wrong foot. But we got into step before our time together ended.

17. Surprise Discoveries

I can't identify any single type of experience as the most difficult ingredient in my grieving. I might make a good case for giving that honor to my loss of Dottie's companionship. I miss being able to share our lives and our love with one another. Another possibility might be encountering familiar objects or activities that provoke a deep sense of loss. Any one of her portraits in my home can tear my heart out so that I feel alone and without hope. I'm not able to choose between these and other candidates for the most painful aspect of mourning.

Recently, though, I have been reminded of the pain produced by another trial during my time of sorrow. I'll call it the shock of surprise discoveries. I have repeatedly happened upon unexpected encounters with realities I have either forgotten or never been aware of. Without advance warning, things come to my attention and re-orient my life. They either expose long-forgotten memories or, more frequently, deepen my understanding and appreciation of Dottie. These discoveries are not so much "re-coveries" as "uncoveries" which disclose life's deeper significance. The incidents are so varied that I can't select any example as typical. I just know that they take me by surprise and pack a powerful emotional wallop. Let me illustrate by recalling the poem "My Father's Hands" which I mentioned earlier. Dorothy had written it as an assignment for one of her graduate courses, and I found it among her papers. She depicted his hands as strong, instructive, quick, loving, severe, exciting, gentle, protective, friendly, beautiful, and trembling. After fifteen years, she remembered them as "still, and still beautiful" in death.

I suppose that I had met LeRoy Pierce, her father, only on a dozen brief visits to his home before his early death. I came to know him mainly through what Dottie said about him over the years. Though he had been a strict master of his home and she could recall at least one severe spanking, she never doubted how much he loved her. She treasured memories of the simple table games they played together in her childhood, and she was proud of steps he took to protect her from danger. Once he banished the town drunk from approaching their Model A Ford, forbidding his use of bad language in the hearing of "my girls." She remembered the comforting safety of his arms after a hunter's stray bullet embedded itself in the wood pile near where she was playing. Her poem was the tender tribute of a grown woman to the father whose love had shaped her life. I knew how much she loved her mother; now I discovered how much she loved her father.

Further, this led to my reconsidering recent changes in Dottie's relationship to me. At her prime, my wife was a strong, self-reliant person who managed household affairs efficiently, allowing me to focus on my ministry. But as her physical and emotional strength declined in recent months, she began to depend more and more on me. The one who had always encouraged me now needed my encouragement. Without realizing it, she was looking to me as a little girl looks to her father. In her closing months, she needed me to cradle her in my arms and love her as she remembered her father loving her. Would it be wrong for me to think that in her poem I had discovered the deeper reason why she often assured me, "I love your hands"?

I was relocating a framed picture from one room to another when I confronted another discovery. The Wives' Fellowship had given this print to her as a farewell gift on our retirement from service at Gordon-Conwell Theological Seminary. In hanging it, I observed that brief notes from well-wishers covered its back. I had forgotten they were there and so paused to read them. All but two or three were from wives of international students, whom she had befriended. She helped them with English as a second language or adjusting to other aspects of American culture. I was aware of her relationship to the girls. In those notes I sensed how much her concern meant to them. Most of them have returned to their home lands, and Dorothy's ministry now extends around the world through them. How little I had comprehended the broad extent of her influence beyond our family—and even our country.

Perhaps the discovery that hit me hardest came very early, so early that it may have been the first to trigger a grief attack. It came when we uncovered small pieces of paper on which Dorothy had jotted brief notes to herself. While the family gathered at the house after her death, one of my children came upon them. The notes were with her prayer list and Bible reading schedule. On one she noted two important facts about herself: "83 years old" and "married 59 years." Another recorded June 2, 1951 as her wedding day and the explanation, "I was married in 1951." Still another listed her birthday "Dot 83 - Sept 2, 2010." Those specifics she wanted to keep in mind.

I knew she feared she might be developing memory problems. She worked at keeping her mind alert by mastering Sudoku puzzles. She determined to maintain her own checkbook and was proud of doing so right up to her final illness. Any confusion over spelling, cooking recipes, appointment dates, or phone numbers upset her. We promised to take care of each other as long as we could, and she seemed to accept my assurance that the Lord would take care of her, even if I were not around. But I suspect that she worried about her memory anyway.

Now these memory-jogging notes testified to her valiant fight to retain vital information she didn't want to lose. They explained the doubts and fears that lay behind her increasing requests for me to take responsibility for duties she had always cared for. So it was I took over mailing out the family greeting cards. This surprise discovery shows that her concern was deeper than I realized. And her bravery greater than I appreciated.

These and other surprise discoveries have opened up new facets of Dottie's life and influence. On one hand, they increase my appreciation for what a wonderful person she was. But on the other, I sense how much I have lost without her at my side. And how far I have fallen short of being the husband she deserved, especially in her times of need. This combination of ingredients nominates these surprise discoveries as a strong candidate for the most painful type of grief.

18. Loneliness at Twilight

It's not as though I had been in isolation all day. Actually, I had spent more time with people than I usually do. At noon I went to lunch with a friend I hadn't seen for several weeks. In mid-afternoon a technician came to the house to repair my computer and we discussed the problem at length. Some other friends, Bill and Phyllis, then entertained me for the evening meal. The food was great, the conversation stimulating, and the time with them well spent. What's that phrase about "the end of a perfect day"?

So I was definitely not prepared for what happened to me as I started home. A completely different mood suddenly settled over me. I puzzled over it for a moment before I heard myself whisper, "I'm lonely." The words came without invitation, from deep within me. They rang true. I really was lonely. In that moment I felt I didn't have a friend in the world.

Until now this sense of abandonment has never crossed my mind. My grief attacks have served as a form of loneliness. Yet they are specific, usually triggered by a particular

event. This evening, however, I felt a vague and overwhelming sense of isolation. It was as though I had been
alone all day even while interacting with other people.
Some who mourn describe this as a routine and pervasive
feeling. Was this mood (which I have been able to avoid so
far) suddenly going to settle over me now?

Why now? Was it because of twilight? That can do it to
me! I recall a ferry trip across Canada's Bay of Fundy years
ago. My young son, Dwight, and I were approaching the
dock at St. Johns, New Brunswick. Our ferry was gliding
slowly over gentle swells. Sunset was giving way to twilight. Crowds waved and called out greetings as we docked.
Yet no one knew we were coming; so none of them were
waiting for us. I can remember how that disheartening lone-
someness felt. Now at this point in my life could the approach of darkness be isolating me from the people whose
presence I needed? I sure hope not, because every day ends
with sunset. I don't want this feeling to remain.

Perhaps I'm entering a new phase of my sorrow. I expected the grieving process to be different, though I cannot
articulate any clear expectations. So I shouldn't be surprised
by any new development in my life. Others in situations
similar to mine have acknowledged their struggle with a
period of loneliness that saps the strength out of them. I've
had brief spells like that, but they have usually passed
quickly. None lingered to depress me.

A few days have passed since my loneliness at twilight.
It did not last long. It has not returned, and I don't know

whether it will. But the possibility has been on my mind, enough so that I have reached my own conclusions about the recent loneliness I experienced. Loneliness may be real but is only, as Rudyard Kipling once said about both Success and Failure, an *imposter*. Loneliness is a psychological reality, as a powerful emotion.

Yet the Christian who feels alone is not in fact alone. The message that loneliness conveys so powerfully to our hearts is false. There is no place in God's creation where we can be alone. "Where can I go from your Spirit? Where can I flee from your presence?" the Psalmist inquired before his Creator. "If I go up to the heavens, you are there; if I make my bed in the depths, you are there" (Psalm 139:7, 8 NIV). Even when we feel most isolated, God is always near—especially to those who call upon him. As we have so often repeated at grave-side services, "Though I walk through the valley of the shadow of death, I will fear no evil; for Thou art with me." Whether I feel lonely or not, when I face life's darkest shadows, God is at my side.

My missionary friend, the late Neil Braun, discovered this truth while mourning the death of his wife, Mary. He stopped in the parking lot to his apartment one evening, trying to muster the strength to enter his house where he would be alone again. Suddenly it was as if he heard God's voice. "Neil, you will not be alone; I am with you." That moment transformed his life. In it he learned the truth he already knew. No matter how lonely any of us may feel, the Lord never leaves us alone. If this loneliness ever comes back, remind me to remember that.

19. Baskets Everywhere

With Dottie's absence, I have introduced several changes in my place to make things more convenient for my new life alone.

For some reason, I felt it necessary to start by assembling my wife's clothing, jewelry, and personal possessions and deciding what to do with them. This has been the hardest of the changes to make. It called up heart-wrenching memories and intensified my sense of how hard it is to go on without her. But, I felt, "This is what she would want me to do." So I viewed my actions with her possessions as agreeing with her desires. As difficult as it was, going through them was necessary and right.

I hit a wall a short time later when I started to gather Dottie's collection of baskets. She and I shared different philosophies on what to do with small items like pencils, note pads, knitting needles, booklets, and other gadgets. My idea was to gather them up and jam them into a space somewhere in a drawer to conceal them. She preferred to find a pretty basket, arrange the items like a bouquet of flowers in it, and display them on a stand or table. It looked like clutter to me, but she took pleasure in it. I wasn't going to make an issue over a few baskets. But now I have started to rearrange the house according to my own preferences.

This meant doing something about those baskets. Although I had become used to them, I was amazed at how they had multiplied. In my five-room house I counted nearly sixty baskets. They varied in size, shape, capacity, height, design and composition. I almost liked some of them. But on general principles I launched a campaign to reduce their numbers drastically. I took secret pleasure in collecting them, emptying them and storing about four dozen (out of sight) in the shed. Finally only a half dozen survived, most of those in the kitchen.

At first I felt satisfied with "restoring order" to the house. The good feeling and pride in a well-done job didn't last long. For one thing, I was left with boxes of things without space in any drawers or cabinets to hide them. For another, when I needed items formerly in the baskets I could not remember where I had hidden them away. For a third, I realized that some of those baskets had actually been attractive. I may have made the house neater, but in the process I made it barren, sterile, drab —almost like a prison cell. I had thrown out the beauty with the baskets and in the process had banished the feminine touch from my home. My Dorothy's touch! I realize now that I should not have acted so hastily.

I began to worry that my triumph over the woven containers might have been an act of betrayal. In getting rid of the baskets I had surely carried a silly difference over how to store things much too far. The baskets had been her means of trying to make our home more convenient and beautiful. Throwing out the baskets now felt like repudiating the most precious person in my life. Why could I not admit even now the value of her way of doing things? What kind of love and loyalty was I showing? I felt worse and worse about those baskets.

My guilt over banishing the baskets may sound ridiculous to you, as it now does to me. But my sorrow reminded me of other disagreements we hadn't reconciled so easily. Like the time when 1 first started to grow a beard, and after about three weeks of scarcely speaking to each other, I shaved it off. Neither of us was happy with the incident. Three years ago when I announced my intention to abandon the beard that had later become my trademark, she asked me not to do so. I felt better and agreed to keep it. Anyway, these baskets are perhaps only one of many instances of sorrow producing an unmerited burden of guilt. (By the way, I will always cherish her request for me to keep my beard.)

The arrival of death in our home has confirmed what I have observed over the years. Grief intertwines with other closely related destructive emotions. Guilt. Anger. Depression. I may have been spared the devastation of anger and depression. But not of guilt, which knows how to torment me with a long series of doubt-raising questions. Had I really been thoughtful and loving to my wife over the years? Had I arranged for her medical treatment as soon as possible after she mentioned being unusually weak? Had I communicated clearly to all of our children the seriousness of her declining condition? Had I authorized only the helpful treatments— and all of them—during Dottie's final illness? I can almost hear Guilt whisper from each one of those exiled baskets another accusing question. Even if I have put those containers out of sight.

20. Whose Kitchen Now?

I approached the kitchen stove with an ice cream scoop in my hand and dropped it into an enameled steel cup behind the burners. That's where Dottie used to keep small metal utensils. Even before turning away I realized it didn't belong there. So I reclaimed it, opened the top cabinet drawer, and put it in its proper place. And then it occurred to me, "This isn't Dorothy's kitchen anymore." Then I took the scoop back and deposited it in the old-fashioned cup again. It now stays where it is most convenient for me.

My ability to do that represents some kind of a milestone in my journey. At first I kept the house the way it had been while she was alive. I left her favorite recliner in the living room with her end table and book case beside it. I was surprised at how hard it was for me to change anything about this spot where Dottie had found so much pleasure in recent years. To remove anything almost felt sacrilegious.

I did take a few things from the table, but not many. And not without some discomfort. After taking care of her clothes, jewelry and personal items, my next major project was sorting through box after box of her keepsakes. We had talked about doing this, but she could not generate any enthusiasm. Those memories made it harder for me, even though I knew I couldn't keep everything. I sorted the items, keeping a few for myself and, passing others on to the children, before I disposed of the rest. But guilt lurked at my shoulder as I let go so many of her prized mementos. It was when I proceeded to clear out the baskets which Dorothy had placed strategically around the house that I felt the worst.

Though time's passage has made it easier to make other changes in our living quarters, altering the kitchen has remained difficult. This was her kitchen, and things were located in the places most convenient for the work she did here. Only when she might be ill or away did I ever disturb anything. I always tried to put items back where they belonged. My memory tells me this has always been her space.

However, with the ice cream scoop I began to make a few intentional changes. Most are designed for my convenience in fulfilling my culinary duties. When my oldest son visited, he commented about finding much more empty space on the counter tops in the kitchen. He was right. I have stored the large electric mixer and its bowls (which I haven't used) and opened up space for mixing scrambled eggs and other new recipe items. Since his mother's death I have come to realize that where you put things in a kitchen depends on what you do and where you do it. Since what

and how I cook is not the same as when she was in charge,
it's only reasonable that changes are required.

And this realization has given me the freedom to alter
placements and patterns in the kitchen without the same attacks of guilt I had after gathering the baskets. I suppose
that my problem with the baskets was that Dottie and I had
disagreed over their propriety. By removing them I was re-
jecting her way of doing things. But we didn't have significant differences over the kitchen. Indeed, I would give anything to have her back cooking again. But there's a new
cook now, and some changes are in order.

Nevertheless, this kitchen stands as a constant reminder
of what a good cook Dorothy was, and of the hours she
slaved in this and previous kitchens to prepare tasty and
economical meals for our children and our many guests
over the years. The guest book on our table bears the signa-
tures of parishioners, students, visiting scholars, missionaries, and other friends—all of which witness her gift of hospitality and kitchen skills. My feeble efforts in this kitchen
magnify by contrast the good things she accomplished here.

I noticed yesterday that a trivet on the wall above the
electric stove still proclaims that this is "Dorothy's
kitchen." I'm in no rush to take it down. In many ways, it's
still her kitchen; not that much has changed. But if you look
carefully while I am in action around mealtime, you will
probably join me in wishing that she were still at work in
this kitchen.

21. Five Month Anniversary

About 10:00 a.m. the truth first hit me: today is the day. The anniversary on my mind for several weeks now has arrived. Dorothy died five months ago today.

Not a single day goes by that I am not conscious of her absence. Most of the time it's a vague, unfocused sense of loss. But not the first day of each month. These anniversaries force me to revisit the numbing shock of watching her final, shallow breath and realizing no others would be coming.

And so the first day of each month provides a focus for my grief, like the magnifying glass I treasured as a boy. That glass concentrated the sun's rays on some blades of dry grass until they burst into flames. And I, that boy now grown, stand equally amazed at the incredible effect of the simple act of remembering. One memory can bring back my helplessness and aloneness, indeed all the impact of grief, concentrating it in one agonizing moment.

In anticipation of the stress of these anniversaries, my emotions draw closer to the surface as each month wears on. For fear of a lump in my throat I dare not mention her name in conversation. My eyes moisten at the glimpse of her photograph. I avoid sitting in her favorite chair. I awaken during the dark hours more often. The first of next month is coming.

This first day thing magnifies the mystery of what we call time. "How long," I ask, "is five months?" Sometimes these months seem so short. Surely it cannot have been a hundred fifty days since from her hospital bed she assured her children not to worry, she was only there for tests! Her hearty smile, her colorful clothing, her zest for being with people, the assurance that she loved me—I have not been without these for five full months, have I? Her death seems more like yesterday.

On the other hand, it has been a very long time. I must have been without her for longer than five months. How else could I have adjusted to sleeping alone, living in such a quiet house, doing the laundry, or eating all by myself? It seems like forever that we have been separated. Without her portraits I can hardly visualize what she looked like. These monthly anniversaries force me to recognize how little I know about myself and the days of my years. I seem to be tossed about by an ocean of time which threatens to drown me whenever I think I understand how long it has been since I saw her last.

Dottie died at 1:30 in the afternoon. On this anniversary I was sharing a late lunch with some friends. I stole glances at my watch as the precise time approached. I knew I couldn't muster the emotional strength to tell them what was on my mind. So the leisurely meal ended and we went our different ways. And then I realized, the time was 1:42 p. m.

The anniversary hour had come and gone without my noticing the exact time. But that's alright. I knew what day it was and I had thought intentionally about Dottie today. And the anguish I had anticipated and feared was not as devastating as I had expected. Maybe the Lord is actually healing my sorrow and life is getting easier. At any rate, I'm sure Dorothy would be proud that I'm able to take care of myself now that I am alone. She had assured me that with God's help I could do that if she were to go first. And for these first five months I have.

Part Four

Progress and Setbacks: Months Eight to Twelve

If months five, six and seven were my hardest they ended with a gradual, almost imperceptible, improvement. I didn't sense it was happening. Perhaps my first clue came when my wedding anniversary, which I had feared would be heart-wrenching, turned out to be less painful than I had foreseen. Anticipating some events was harder than experiencing them. With time I became aware further that the frequency and intensity of my grief attacks were slowly diminishing. My progress was not smooth; there were occasional and painful setbacks. I now recognize that my writing pattern was also changing. I found fewer noteworthy encounters to record and felt less urge to write about them. Whereas, I had written passionately about painful incidents I now found fewer experiences that would stir me to write. The focus of my attention was also shifting. I had been absorbed with myself, how bad I felt and how much I had lost. I began to see how self-centered my sorrow had made me. Dorothy remained in my thoughts, but slowly she was appearing as a person in her own right. I started to develop my understanding of who Dorothy was and what she had accomplished. I had been viewing her as the cause of my sadness, but in these months I came to appreciate her as a person who lived faithfully for God to the end of her days. I saw her no longer as one whose life had been cut short, but as a child of God who had completed the entire course God had set before her.

22. Is My House Still a Home?

Fifteen years have passed now since Dorothy and I moved into our new Florida house. In spite of the usual frustrations while unpacking and placing our furnishings, the new structure slowly became our *home*. It remained our *home* until her death last autumn left me as the single occupant of the building.

I wasn't sure what lay ahead. Not since I had lost my mother thirty years earlier has death touched me so personally. "I don't know," I would tell my children when they pressed their inquiries about my future plans, "I have never passed this way before." I assured them that I didn't intend to make quick decisions, but I had few if any helpful details about what they might expect.

Behind their curiosity and my vague replies lay a common concern. Would I want to continue living alone in the house their mother and I had shared for fifteen years? For me the issue quickly resolved into another: Would this place continue to be my *home* or would it go back to being just a house?

As one of Robert Frost's characters observed, "It all depends on what you mean by home." Poets and novelists have led the effort to define that word home. Since I don't belong to either of those groups I dare not insert myself too much into the debate. Yet since I've brought up the question of whether my living space is still a *home*, maybe I need to explain what I mean by the word. Home denotes to me a place where a person experiences a peace and well being, which in turn produces a feeling of comfort and belonging. A home is the place where you fit without undue stress or tension. I know that's not much of a definition, but that's OK because I suspect it's more important for a home to be experienced than for it to be defined. For me, a home is where you feel at home.

Now you can see why broken hearted people might wonder whether they could ever again experience the comfort and well being necessary to make a home. That's exactly the uncertainty that overwhelmed me as I drove back from the hospital following Dottie's death. My first surprise when I entered the house was that it still seemed to be the same place. Nothing had changed. Furniture, appliances, dishes, and pictures—all were where I had left them. No dark mist of gloom smothering the rooms. Not even Dottie's absence overcame me at first. (Perhaps a part of me was expecting her to re-appear from another room.) Not even the gradual arrival of other family members made things appear too strange or unreal.

Naturally, coming home was only the beginning. Before me lay the task of doing something with her clothing and other personal possessions. Then I would have to search for legal documents among her other papers, letters and souvenirs—all wrapped, as it turned out, in tear-provoking memories. Soon I would rearrange things for my convenience— even though it felt like betraying Dorothy to move anything. And seeing every portrait or family photo in the house would tear at my heart and call forth tears.

But I had determined I wasn't going to hide away in this place and feel sorry for myself. Even without Dottie, I would go where we had gone together and keep up what had been our outside schedule of activities: church, shopping, visiting friends, eating out, attending funerals—you name it. All too quickly I found this was more difficult than I expected. At the house I could groan and weep when I had to; but out in public no one wants anyone to rain on their party. I needed to heed my mother's advice during my childhood to be on my best behavior whenever I went out. I had to be careful what topics I brought up, to breathe deeply before I replied to some questions, and to brace up for those grief attacks which could be waiting to ambush me.

With time I realized that going home was actually a relief from those pressures in the outside world. Dorothy's absence continues to devastate me, and the reality is this isn't going to change. Her pictures and everything around me still stir memories that steal my sense of well being. Yet when I dry my eyes and muscle my way through the sor-

row, I find something else. Sad memories can become win-
dows through which to see again the wonderful times
spread through our nearly sixty years of marriage. I can recall joys long lost sight of in the busy-ness of the passing
years. Strange as it may seem, not having her physical presence in the house today enables me to rescue her from a
yesterday that has stolen so much of our shared experience.

When C. S. Lewis' wife, Joy, was dying of cancer they
visited a beautiful country valley. Sensing his sadness, she
offered this encouragement, "The pain then is part of the
pleasure now." After her death, Professor Lewis returned to
that same spot with Joy's young son to encourage the grieving boy with the insight that "The pleasure then is part of
the pain now." In a similar way, Dottie and I knew that the
joys we shared could not last in this life. They were all
tinged in the painful truth that death would inevitably break
the union made by the promises of our youth. The day
when death did us part has arrived and, I will try to reclaim
from within today's pain sweet memories of the happiness I
shared with her yesterday. And I can do so in this building
that we called *home*.

In another way, her absence communicates Dorothy's
continuing presence within me. In the silence of my house,
I hear again her long forgotten words of encouragement,
the unmerited but so uplifting compliments, and the expressions of confidence that have strengthened me throughout
my life. I miss my greatest fan, but somehow from every
room of the house I hear the wife of my youth cheer me on.

And maybe it is actually because she is no longer here that this house—which once was ours together—remains my retreat from life's stresses, the place where I belong, and one of God's means of comforting me at this time in my life.

Come to think of it, isn't that what I said I thought a *home* was?

23. Thoughts by a Grave

I went by Dottie's grave this afternoon.

I have probably only visited it a dozen times or so in the six months since her burial. I don't avoid going because I fear being overcome with sorrow. Nor do I feel drawn there in the expectation that somehow I will be closer to her at that spot. I sometimes sense a bit of guilt that I don't experience the deep emotional reactions others report about their visits to family plots.

I'm not sure how to describe what happens to me when I stand there. Part of me is buried in that earth. No one needs to remind me of that. In that sense I know a deep sadness. It was intense on one early visit when I attended a grave side service at a nearby plot. I could look beyond the casket as it was being lowered into the ground and catch sight of Dottie's grave in the background. As our small assembly thinned, I observed a recently bereaved friend at the spot where he had laid his wife to rest. He went alone; later so did I. We kept our composure. Neither of us wanted to make conversation.

Our stone marker hasn't been delivered yet. But when it comes it will bear the words from the King James Bible to which Dorothy had returned in recent years, "He giveth his beloved sleep" (Ps.127:2). The words come to mind when I go to that spot. She rests from her labors here, delivered from pain and suffering, and safe in the arms of Jesus. I expect to join her. This truth keeps me from plunging into despair. Since it is from this spot I expect both of us to rise immortal when our Lord returns in triumph, I know I am not now as close to her here as I will be then. Maybe the biblical comparison of death to sleep and its promise of a future resurrection affects my feelings more than others might expect.

Still I return on occasion to the spot. Most of the time I come because I want her resting place to look nice. The soil is sandy. Only a little grass has grown in from the sides of the rectangular site where she lies. I watch with genuine interest for each new blade to appear and to be sure the rest of the lawn doesn't grow too high. As Easter approached, I placed eight small plants, the flowers of each with white petals framing a crimson center, at the head of her grave. And on Easter my daughter and I added a lily with which a friend had memorialized Dorothy at church that morning. Keeping that small space looking nice is one of the few things I can still do for her.

In the last church I served before retiring, I shared several burials with a funeral director who would have made a wonderful pastor. "The living," he reminded me one day, "must bury their own dead." By that he meant we cannot hold on to loved ones who die but must accept the fact of their deaths. Maybe that's really what brings me back to Dottie's grave. Standing there, I acknowledge she is gone. I accept the painful reality of her death. Standing there, I cannot deny the great loss in my heart. Standing there, I accept her death, re-commit her to God's care, and trust in the future reality of her resurrection.

I went to her grave this afternoon. But not for the last time.

24. Sixty Years Ago Today

It was a hot, humid, cloudy day in Maine sixty years ago today. The previous evening Dorothy and I had been busy, but had purchased some free time by promising ourselves "We can do that in the morning." Well, morning came and raced by so quickly that we had no chance to do everything we had left undone. Especially as we had to stay away from each other so we could avoid the dire consequences of the groom seeing his bride before the ceremony.

Surprisingly, our 2 p. m. wedding finally got underway only ten minutes late (even if the flowers never got placed inside the church). The small auditorium had only standing room left when the brides first made their appearance. I say "brides" because we were married in a double wedding ceremony featuring two home town girls who had been college classmates. Several parts of the service—including the exchange of vows and rings—had to be administered twice. Combine that with a hot, humid day inside a packed house and you can probably feel my vivid memory of perspiration streaming down my back under that formal black tuxedo.

The photography, reception, opening of gifts, and our twilight departure in my 1936 Chevrolet sedan have since merged into one confused memory. But today—sixty years later—I still remember clearly the joy of that wonderful day when Dottie and I entrusted ourselves to each other. However, today I must face my first anniversary without her at my side. My family and friends have been concerned about how difficult I might find it. Me, too.

At 7:45 a. m. (the time she and I customarily ate our breakfast together) I sat at the kitchen table. In my opening prayer, I again thanked God for those fifty-nine plus years he had put her in my care and for the multitude of blessings included in those years. I meant each word I spoke; yet simply putting my gratitude into words opened the flood-gate of my sorrow. I do not cry so often now; even though I do not miss her less as time passes. My tears do not under-mine the gratitude I have; they underline it. My sadness in the present is a tribute of appreciation for the gift of her love and support which have blessed my life in the past. The Lord has given and now he has taken away; I will still bless his name.

I received one anniversary card in the mail from friends who knew me well enough to rejoice with me over these many years of the good marriage God gave us. They under-stood (as I now also do) how nice it is to have friends re-member the special days in your life.

Later another good friend and I drove to Dottie's grave where I showed him the newly-arrived granite stone and we watered the memorial flowers beside her name. I neither felt unusually close to her at that spot nor did I feel unusual remorse. She is in God's keeping, and so am I. That's true here, and also true wherever I go. I miss her; but I will not forget her.

Mid-afternoon I hunted up our Wedding Album. Usually we couldn't locate it for our anniversaries; but having recently gone through Dottie's collection of valued things, I knew right where it was. So I studied each 8x10 with care. You can do that when you have only a dozen. Sixty years is over a half century; no wonder that young bride and groom don't look familiar to me. Yet, I have no difficulty recognizing their joy on that special day. And I almost think that I can feel it again for I have relived it in a thousand experiences since then. I thank God for these pictures to keep my memories fresh.

Only my best man, Cushman Bryant, and I are alive from my wedding party. His anniversary is in mid-June and in recent years we two couples have celebrated together. So tonight Cush, his wife Erlene, and I visited a new restaurant in the nearby city of Live Oak together. We had a great meal and a wonderful time. Our conversation allowed for memories of previous meals together going back to this day sixty years ago.

Beside me was the empty chair where in the past Dottie
would have sat. A year ago we four celebrated in a Japanese
restaurant in Valdosta, Georgia. But now there were only
three of us. And from time to time, I glanced at the chair
and thought of Dorothy. How I miss her. At the same time I
was able to retain my composure and to thank God that of
these sixty years, he let me have her for all but these past
seven months. How much he has blessed me. That's what
I'm really celebrating today.

25. Baskets and Beauty

By now I have made good progress in remaking my home according to my own preferences. You may remember that my efforts to do so began with my campaign against Dottie's baskets. I exiled most of them to the shed, gave a few away, and now only a handful remain in the house.

Yet, as I have already confessed, I began to have second thoughts about the baskets even before proclaiming my victory over them. With time's passage I came to realize that many of her baskets were attractive as well as useful. How could I have lived with them over the years and not realized it? They weren't simply containers, but glimpses of beauty, the sight of which lifted your spirit as you moved around our home.

You might conclude that by now most of them would have regained their earlier places in my home. Not exactly. I have deliberately reinstated a few of them; but, my further thought about those woven containers has led me in a different direction. It has prompted me to contemplate the

many different ways Dottie brought beauty into our home.
We both grew up during America's Great Depression; she
within a large family in a country village, and I in a factory
city as son of a widow on welfare. What beauty my home
contained came from the music in my mother's fingers and
voice. Dorothy's home abounded in good country cooking
and in other forms of beauty produced by masters of crafts
passed down from mothers to their daughters.

So after Dottie and I married I was spared the trials of eating the cooking of a bride inexperienced in the kitchen. Instead, she introduced me from the outset to more beautiful
meals than those I knew in my own childhood home. Un-
like my mother, Dorothy never attempted vocal solos and
did not play a musical instrument. Yet her fingers had ac-
quired the accumulated family skills which enabled her to
create "all things bright and beautiful," whether in the
kitchen or elsewhere in our home.

And this is what the exiled baskets called back into my
mind—her eye for beauty and the amazing ability of her
fingers to produce lovely things. Not that she built the baskets—as far as I know she didn't make a single one of
them. But she saw how they could combine utility and
loveliness in our home. So from the early days of our marriage I saw her do precisely that as I watched her agile fingers produce loveliness by processes I did not even know
how to name. She could sew, crotchet, knit, tat, embroider,
do cross-stitch and later cover plastic canvass.

I recall the bright kitchen curtains that appeared as we settled into our first home. Then how she crafted delicate clothing and warm flannel blankets for the arrival of our first child. Later I stood amazed at the afghans, warm winter scarves and spectacularly bright woolen sweaters she made for her family. Her intricately designed tablecloths and doilies appeared to adorn our wooden furniture tops. Over the entire span of our marriage she displayed more talent and thoughtfulness than I ever dreamed she could have. She lovingly sowed a crop of beauty from which we harvested a lifetime of blessing. Many of these items (I wish I knew how many) were tenderly wrapped and delivered to greet new babies or to wish neighbors a "Merry Christmas." When we were approaching retirement age and living among student families at the seminary where I taught, she took courses in quilting to add still another means to make our world more beautiful and to encourage young wives to nurture their talents.

In recent years, though, arthritis invaded her fingers to limit their mobility and its pain denied her the privilege of using the skills which had given her so much joy. And now she has left me surrounded by the beauty she created to brighten our home. Somewhere there is even a small pillow with the announcement, "**The Deans**, established 1951."

I have no difficulty believing that God was working through her, for it is he who beautifies this marred and broken world in which we live. Who but the Lord can accomplish what the ancient prophet promised, "[He will] comfort all who mourn [and] ... bestow on them a crown of beauty instead of ashes" (Isa 61:2, 3)?

Maybe Dottie's baskets have not yet regained their former prominence in my home. But they have triggered one of the most precious blessings which rises out of my sadness: the opportunity to think back over her life and to observe how many ways she left this world a more beautiful place than she had found it. And as I continue to live in it, this is a part of her legacy to me.

26. Do I . . . or, Did I?

At first, I found it difficult to use the correct tense
when I talked about Dottie. Once she died I should, of
course, have spoken about her in some form of a past tense.
Instead of saying, "She always *called* her brother by his
nick-name, 'Haddie'," I would hear myself say, "She *calls*
her older brother 'Haddie'..." Sometimes I realized that I
was speaking incorrectly, but most of the time I was bliss-
fully unaware of the mistake.

Force of habit was tricking me into using the present
tense. That's how I had spoken about her since she first
came into my life. So it was natural to keep on talking that
way. Yet maybe my problem was deeper than mere habit.
Talking about my wife in the present tense might have re-
vealed how very much I wanted her back with me. Sure, I
knew she was dead. I had seen her draw her last breath. I
had followed her casket to the cemetery. However, a part of
me still didn't want to accept that reality. If only this terri-
ble situation were merely a bad dream, and I'd awaken to

find that It hadn't really happened! I wouldn't have admitted it, but sometimes I half expected her to appear in any room where I might be. I struggled with a "disconnect" between what I knew was true and what with all my heart I wanted to be true. I know this disconnect sounds irrational. With good reason; it is!

It came slowly; but gradually the finality of Dorothy's death did permeate my life. A hospice counselor noticed when she no longer detected any expectation that Dottie might reappear any day. And as I began to accept that I was going to be without her for the rest of this life I found myself using the past tense more frequently and more consistently. And now I am not aware of using the present tense concerning her at all.

Except for one situation. I wonder which is correct for me to say: "I love her (present)" or only that "I loved her (past)"? My problem is not just grammatical, although I know tense is part of grammar. It is also emotional, because it burrows into my deepest feelings. I keep an 8x10 full color portrait of Dottie on the desk where I begin each day with my Scripture reading. When I sit down my eyes search her face for any opportunity to refresh my memory of our shared life. She is as precious to me now as she has ever been. The words, punctuated by tears, come unbidden to my lips, "I love you, I still love you. I still love you." And I still do.

The present tense is all right in this case—at least, as far as the statement is about me. Right now, I still do love her. She occupies no less a place in my heart than she did while alive. I cannot now do anything to make her life any easier; but I would make an even greater effort to do so if it were possible. For grief has shown me my past failures and forced me to suffer my share of guilt. It is true, I still do love her.

But, can I still love *her*? Can my love be love if it is not received? Can I love someone who is no longer here to be loved? And can my love really be love if it does not do her any good? The problem is no longer grammatical, nor is it just emotional. Since God has always been central to our relationship the issue is theological. If God so loved the world that he gave his one and only Son to save sinners, then that love is as genuine towards those who do not receive it as it is to anyone else. If God can love those who do not respond to or return his love, why can't I? The most troubling aspect is the question whether I can still love my wife if she is no longer here. If, as I believe, she is asleep in death, and can neither know of my love nor benefit from it, then can I still love her?

I take solace from the biblical reminder that as a believer she is "asleep in Jesus" (1 Thess 4:14) and that not even death can separate her from God's love in Christ (Rom 8:38, 39). Death may be an enemy, but physical death has not destroyed my wife's existence. She continues to be since she is asleep in Christ and safely bound to

God's love. Even as years ago I whispered my love to our infant daughter asleep in her mother's arms—though our baby knew it not, so now I am free to tell her mother of my love as she sleeps even more peacefully in Jesus' care. While she may not knowingly benefit from my love now, she will one day know that I have demonstrated my love for her by loving our family and others for whom she cared deeply. This will mean so much to her when we are united again in the resurrection.

So never mind the problems with the grammar. I will continue to affirm both statements. I did love my wife. And I still do!

27. Little Girl from Maine

As the most painful phase of my sadness has lessened, my attention has shifted away from me and my loss to consider instead the significance of Dorothy's now completed life. More and more I come to view her not as one whose life was cut short (my loss), but as a servant of our Lord who completed her life in faithfulness to him (Christ's gain, Philip 1:21).

So it was that one day I was thinking back to her funeral and how Pastor John Harper had highlighted the importance of world missions in Dottie's life. I don't think I had ever looked at her story from that viewpoint; but, his words encouraged me to try to find that missionary thread stretching through a whole lifetime.

I took my starting point in Dottie's often expressed surprise at the contrast between her humble birth in a small New England village and the international horizons of her

later life. To underline her gratitude, she would often challenge people to consider what God had done for "this little
girl from Maine."

My guess is that her first exposure to the world missionary enterprise came during that little girl's pre-school
childhood. During the shortages of America's Great Depression her parents sent her to live with her Uncle Syke
and Aunt Harriet. There at their dinner table she first met
missionaries to faraway places, for whom she later prayed
regularly. So began her life-long practice of prayer for missionaries. Her childhood pastor had inherited a missionary
interest from his own father who was mastermind of India
operations for the small Bible Faith Mission (1911-1939).

When, as a teen, Dottie accepted Christ as savior, she
did so under the preaching of Rev. H. L. Faulkingham, director of another world mission agency. The next pastor of
her church was president of that same mission board over-
seeing missionaries in Asia. The monthly missionary prayer
letter he published deepened her prayer life.

So it was she brought this missionary interest from her
Maine childhood with her to the small college in metropoli-
tan Boston which we both entered in 1947. At this hot bed
of world mission enthusiasm the two of us joined the popu-
lar campus club, the Student Foreign Mission Fellowship.
The SFMF's annual missionary conference featured enthu-
siastic speakers who challenged students to become mis-

sionaries. Many of our classmates and friends did go overseas. Dottie was chair of the club's 1950 missionary conference. By then she had already decided to go wherever God
wanted her to go. As a matter of fact, so had I. We agreed
that wherever God might send us we would go together.

Not surprisingly that would be to another country. We
were newlyweds in June, 1951 when we crossed the Cana-
dian border to spend the next six years in the village of
Danville, Quebec. We did not then think of ourselves as
missionaries, but we should have. Two unfamiliar cultures
surrounded us: that of militant French nationalists who ad-
vocated separating from Canada's national government,
and an English population that reflected the reserve and tra-
ditionalism of its British sympathies. We struggled with
how we as foreigners could present Christ and his claims
effectively to Canadians.

The world missionary concern of our congregation
warmed Dorothy's heart. The ladies mission society provided a monthly missionary program for our whole church.
Based on her college experience, Dottie helped the church
organize and conduct several mission conferences. She also
tested her cooking talents on visiting missionaries.

Here she and I first learned of Ponmar, India, a village
where our people had a sister church. Danville had paid for
the construction of Ponmar's first church building and for
about thirty years had helped to finance its operation. Our

people inspired Dorothy and me into our own lifelong interest in that faraway congregation. At the same time we encouraged the preparation of one of our church youth for missionary service. Miss Luvia Webb was already studying at *L'Ecole Biblique Bethel* in nearby Sherbrooke. Her burden was to reach French-speaking Canadians. Dottie and Luvia prayed together and exchanged advice and encouragement. Dottie followed Luvia's missionary work throughout her life. In Danville Dorothy learned that you do world missions right where you are, and also through others wherever they are—in India or in Quebec.

When In 1957 I became pastor of the Blessed Hope Church in Springfield, Massachusetts, Dottie met Bernice Russell, a public health nurse who had been born of missionary parents in Africa's Congo. Bernice exemplified complete dedication to world missions. As a member of the missionary society Dottie also helped with missionary conferences and entertaining their visiting speakers, who now also included overseas national workers and missionary candidates. By this time her home itself had become a mission field with our five children (Plus a series of seven foster children) needing to learn about Jesus. She brought world missions into our home life through Scripture, prayer, missionary biographies, and entertaining visitors from afar. Miss Barbara White, one of our church members, helped missions come alive for our church as she prepared to leave for India. Dottie led a delegation (including our children) to the airport to witness her departure.

Her missionary horizons enlarged again in 1964 when I joined the faculty at Berkshire Christian College in Lenox, Mass. Surrounded by energetic youth who were eager to reach the world, she helped to finance several in their missionary internships and short term trips overseas. The annual missionary conference recharged her batteries. But now the student body included Christians from India, Uganda, Switzerland, and Japan—to mention a few. As she entertained these in our home they became our children's friends, and hers as well. And gradually Dottie realized the tremendous potential in missions of preparing and utilizing national workers.

Later when I taught at Gordon-Conwell Theological Seminary (1991-96), we lived in campus housing among numerous international student families. The world had come to her doorstep. She hosted visiting European and Asian scholars and offered families visiting from overseas their first meal in an American home. She tutored student wives in English and helped Oriental mothers and American public school teachers understand each other. And she became more convinced than ever of the potential for these nationals to impact their own societies for Christ when they returned home.

It fascinates me to realize that my wife ("this little girl from Maine") passed through the same changes in her commonsense missionary philosophy that Christianity's leading missiologists were developing—and at roughly the same time. Together they were learning how much both Scripture and our changing world require that western missionaries must work in partnership with national Christian workers to proclaim and apply the gospel to their own lands. Dottie had entered her own commitment to indigenization, contextualization, and networking before she ever heard those technical terms. She had to wait for my retirement before she could apply her new perspective to work in other cultures. We made our first trip to Asia in 1997 to serve as volunteer teachers at Indian Theological Seminary in Chennai, India. While I taught theological subjects, Dottie taught English as a second language. She quipped about the irony of a "girl with a Maine accent teaching British English to Asian students;" but she did her best. She felt that she made her greatest contribution in teaching students how to read the Bible in public. This had become her idea of missionary work: to equip nationals for the work of ministry.

While in India, she frequently recounted in public services how God had healed her of a brain tumor, thus permitting her trip to India. Following services in which she shared her story, people would line up to have her pray for them. Dottie counseled with two of the older girls in a children's home where we were housed.

Her responsibilities were lighter when later we taught in the Philippines. While we did entertain college students for meals in our home, her main task was to tutor two daughters of missionaries Jeff and Penny Vann. She also went with me twice on shorter trips to Japan; where her principle involvement was encouraging those she met. In one English conversation class she gave her testimony. And she even got to visit one of the seminary wives to whom she had taught English back in America. Our final trip outside the USA took us to Mexico's Baja peninsula. While I was teaching at a pastors' retreat, Dottie spent much of her time with an overworked missionary wife. They both valued their friendship, and Dottie never forgot her Mexico ministry.

So when I look back upon Dorothy's life, I can see that Pastor John had more insight than I had realized. Dorothy Dean had lived world missions as a central theme of her life.

Her story makes that clear; but it leaves much unsaid. It misses a young co-ed's perplexity over where God wanted her to serve. It omits her motherly concern while anxiously awaiting mail from her sixteen year old daughter on a summer mission to Hispaniola. It overlooks a grandmother's willing sacrifice of the early childhood years of her first granddaughter whose missionary dad took her with him to the Philippines. Unseen also was her love for an infant great granddaughter (whom she never would get to hold in her arms) living in China with her missionary parents. Equally hidden from view are the tear stained lists of missionary needs over which she prayed daily. Largely unseen too are the many lifelong friends she worked with in women's mission societies. Her story only hints at how much world missions filled her heart.

Perhaps we both felt Dorothy's missionary spirit most meaningfully in 1998 while visiting a hilltop church in Ponmar, India. There we two Americans stood before a bronze tablet expressing the gratitude of an Indian church to our Danville congregation. In our hearts we were returning again to the little church in Canada where we had begun life together. At the twilight of our ministry in a land far from home we felt anew the excitement we had known at its dawn—we were now as then right where God wanted us to be—involved in telling the world about Jesus.

I like to think that moment summarizes both Dottie's heart for world missions and the story of my life with "this little girl from Maine." I can see better now what a truly wonderful story it was.

28. My Lakeside Cabin

As I approach the first anniversary of my life as a widower, I find fewer memorable situations to write about. I take more interest in daily life, spend less time looking back and do more planning ahead. My grief attacks are less frequent and less intense. In addition, they pass more quickly. I think less often about me and my feelings, and think more about Dorothy and the meaning of her life. Grief is springing fewer surprises on me, and I seem to be more comfortable with my "new normal."

In August I made my first trip alone back to our summer cottage in Maine. I expected to confirm how well I was recovering from sorrow, and I hoped to gather evidence that the acute stage of my grief was over.

Now after a month on a hillside overlooking picturesque Lake Messalonskee, my venture draws to a close. I am disappointed. Sorrow still hides behind each reawakened memory. It still emerges at the most inconvenient times to disrupt my life. My return appears to have set back my progress almost to those early days right after Dorothy's funeral.

At home I had adjusted to her absence from my life. Most of her personal items are gone, or at least out of sight. I no longer expect her to appear—or speak to me—from another room. I have adjusted to doing things my way. Here at our cottage, though, she has always been at my side. I still want her with me, just as she used to be. Once again I miss her more than I can put into words

Daily I see her favorite books and glance at a rack full of the coffee mugs she collected.

Her empty chair is at the table for every meal and her side of the bed is always unoccupied. My emotions are once again just beneath the surface. These are all repeats of the start of my sorrows almost a year ago in Florida.

But let me share some details of my month-long stay at the camp where she and I have relaxed for much of each summer since my retirement. The testing started as I first entered the cottage. My wife inevitably feared how much damage our off-season residents (field mice, chipmunks, bats, etc.) might have done during our absence. Once inside, I searched in vain for nests in the sofa bed, stores of acorns on kitchen shelves, or holes gnawed in our mattresses.

I was thrilled to find that our summer home appeared to be in better shape than we had usually found it. So thrilled that I wanted to tell her. And it was back, that instinctive need to share with her this happy news. Instead of ushering me into a communion of joy, my new setting reawakened my pain at being alone. At home I had become accustomed to her absence; but to be without her here was a new experience. It resembled the old one.

I remembered I had left some clothing in the cabin, but couldn't recall what or where. I soon found some of my work clothes in a drawer and beside them a pair of Dottie's slippers. At a glance I recognized them as her favorite pair. Stylish. Comfortable. Wearable both inside and outdoors. They provoked my first tears of the trip. She would never have left those slippers here if she had suspected she would not return. Nor had I anticipated when we left that I would have to come back alone. Suddenly I was looking not at slippers, but at the brevity and uncertainty of life. My mortality as well as hers. As Scripture says, my times—like Dorothy's—are in God's hands (Ps 31:15). Grief's dark gloom and sadness were back with me; but now I mourned for me as much as for her.

I faced another heartbreaker when I began to find her Post-it notes stuck to various items throughout the cottage. These were all done in the impeccable penmanship of the seasoned third-grade teacher with whom I had lived. I recognized her handwriting easily. Dorothy had been a planner, one who constructed lists of things to be done, and drew up instructions for doing them. (I would often jokingly accuse her of being more interested in planning a trip

than in taking it. It was a charge she denied; but I did have
a point.)

Like clues on a scavenger hunt, her notes told me what
was stored where (e. g., salt and pepper shakers in the bread
box, or blankets in an upstairs barrel) or warned about possible problems (e.g., don't turn the refrigerator down or the
eggs will freeze).

At first, it was as if she were speaking to me from the
grave; later I realized she who had feared her memory was
faltering had probably written these as reminders to herself.
But whether intended for me or for her, she was not here—
and I had no human companion. Reading a note is no sub-
stitute for talking with a person. My sorrow was back.

But now my month-long return draws to a close and I
sense that the pain is probably lessening. My grief attacks
are again less frequent and don't disturb me as much. Or
last as long. One particular experience confirmed that they
have eased into the background. The annual meeting of our
Camp Meeting Association memorialized Dorothy in a res-
olution of appreciation. Normally I would have fought back
the tears. But this time a feeling of pride overwhelmed me.
What she had done for the cause at Lakeside was only a
small part of her contributions over the years. The important consideration at that moment was not how much I
had lost, but how much Christ has gained through her long
and faithful life. I realized that I have made progress.

In a way this journey stands as a microcosm of the ten-month-long course of my sadness. In a single month I have re-arranged my dwelling and my life to compensate for Dottie's absence. I have adjusted to her not being here. What used to be her cabin now bears more of my imprint. I have replaced vivid memories of our life together in this place with fresh experiences of God's grace to a man who feels all alone.

Whether here or in Florida, I can sense the same subtle shift. My memories of Dottie in both locations were at the start both vivid and painful, perhaps even more painful because they were so vivid. The passage of time has eased the pain of those memories, partially replacing them with a new awareness of God's presence, even in her absence. You might even say that I have traded the pain of my vivid recollections of my life with her for new memories of God's presence during my lonely hours without her. As my pain decreased and my memories of her became less prominent so also my awareness of God's presence has increased.

Here in our summer cottage it is as though God has once again used my sense of his abiding nearness almost as a sedative to ease the burden of my sorrow. Yet I also sense a trade-off. The more real he becomes to me now the more my memories of Dorothy recede into the past. Maybe I should view this as an exchange of the pain of her absence for the pleasure of knowing God's companionship when I need him so much.

I can almost discern an analogy in what happened during her final hospitalization. When Dottie's pain intensified our family joined her in an urgent request for medication to provide relief. After the anti-pain treatments took effect we saw no further evidence that she was suffering. But with her deliverance from pain came also the loss of her ability to communicate with us anymore. She may have heard what we said, but she never spoke to us again. Perhaps in a similar exchange those of us who grieve must also be prepared to surrender our most vivid memories in order to escape our most acute pain. Maybe the price of our healing is the dimming of our memories of the person we miss.

But now autumn approaches and I return to Florida. I go back with no delusions that my sorrow is all in the past. I do return, though, with the awareness that I have come a long way even if I still have a distance yet to go. I have honored Dorothy by going back to the place where we spent many happy hours. She would have wanted me to do that. The trip has not been easy and the grief over her absence rests more heavily on my heart. But I rejoice at renewing the good memories of wonderful times together. I do not want to lose them. If God will keep her memory alive for me, I should be willing to accept the sorrow that comes with it.

29. Would-Have-Been Birthday

$\mathbf{A}$s September 2011 began my children and I were as widely scattered as the end of summer usually makes inevitable. As far as I know, no two households of us were together. Yet we were all united in a common inability to wish Dorothy Dean "Happy Birthday." After speaking to a couple of my children by phone, I sent off this email to them all.

To our Family,

Today Mother would have been eighty-four years of age, and I am fully aware that (even while we are separated by many miles) we are all united in a keen awareness of that reality. Each one of us faces the same frustration of not being able to communicate our love to her on this her special day.

Of course, this desire to share something with her is not confined to the ability to say "Happy Birthday!" I often look at her picture and say "I love you." I know she cannot hear me; but I have to say it because...I still do love her. And you share that same cherished love, heightened by our isolation from one another. I have already heard from some of you and want to reassure you that you are not alone in your sorrow. That every one of you will feel that way provides all the more reason for you to contact one another today.

Today is even harder than you may have expected for we've been without her for ten months now. The daily sense of pain no longer haunts us as it did at first. But our sorrow has diminished only because she is no longer in the forefront of our minds. We have not forgotten her; yet life has become easier for us by not having her so often consciously in our thoughts. So when days like this bring her back into our minds so forcefully let us accept the jolt as God's way of reminding us not to forget your mother and all the blessings she brought into our lives. So don't be ashamed of your tears today. Mother is worthy of every one of them.

And don't stop there. Push right on through this curtain of sorrow and relive the good times we celebrated with her on birthdays past. It was then that we did communicate with her and expressed our love as best we could. Today is a day of wonderful memories. Dust them off and enjoy them again. "This is the day the Lord has made; let us rejoice and be glad in it" (Psalm 118:24).

As for me I plan to celebrate today, and I urge you to do likewise. It need not be a hilarious party. But set apart some time today for remembering your mother. Relive the last time you were together for her birthday. Forget this day without her and rejoice in her coming new birth day when our Lord Jesus returns to reunite us as a family. She loved us to the end of her earthly life; and she will yet love us again. For my part, I have arranged to have some of her special friends (Judy and Bill Willard) join me for dinner at a restaurant in nearby Madison. Our meal will be quiet and subdued and I will not be able to say as much as I should like. Nonetheless, your mother will be foremost in my thoughts. I hope you will find some way to celebrate that fits you and yours. We want everyone to understand that we do not sorrow like people who have no hope.

With all my love, D A D

This of course, wasn't the last thought I gave to this day. Birthdays are the milestones by which we number our days and measure life's progress. I cannot believe now that I was not more conscious that Dorothy's days were numbered, and my time with her was nearing its close. Common sense should have told me that. And even if it had not, Scripture itself is explicit:

"The years of our life are seventy,
Or even by reason of strength eighty;
Yet their span is but toil and trouble;
They are soon gone, and we fly away."
- Psalm 90:10 (ESV)

Dottie had already enjoyed her eighty years and they were soon gone. Birthdays are signposts pointing all of us to the fragile beauty and brevity of life. So may I and all who know about this would-have-been birthday "number our days that we may get a heart of wisdom" (Ps 90:12, ESV).

30. Nine White Roses

Nine beautiful white flowers. I deliberately walked over to my tallest Confederate Rose bush to count them. There were more than I had suspected at first glance. All nine were gorgeous in the late September sun. It's noon time and these blossoms are at their best. Pure white. About six inches across. Looking outwards, as if to receive the compliments of any passing spectators. I would gladly have offered one—if there were someone to listen. But I'm not about to talk to the bush and its blossoms. And my wife is not here anymore.

Once again I miss Dorothy. She was the kind of person who loved beauty wherever she found it. Especially beautiful flowers! Being a frugal New Englander, I didn't shower flowers on her. (I now wish I had sent them more often.) But, in fact these flowers had been my gift to her. I who have no "green thumb" had put the small branches into the ground and watered them until they became this large bush, now towering above my head. And when each bud blossomed, I used to call it to her attention. She would often view them from our kitchen window. Now she's gone. But our Confederate Roses still bloom.

Dottie would have loved this moment. As she drank in their beauty we could have talked about these flowers. She was home several years ago when I brought in a dozen cuttings that a friend had given me. We both doubted whether these dried-up branches could ever amount to anything. But in the spring I dutifully stood them in water. She was as surprised as I when they somehow took root and sprang to life. In autumn she was fascinated by their ability to change color through the day. If she were here now Dottie would have talked on about these nine flowers, and shared our enjoyment.

We had never even heard about the Confederate Rose before we moved south to Florida. They tell me the bush is not really a rose; and I can confirm that it doesn't look or act like any other roses I've seen. It has no detectable fragrance and no thorns; but its flowers are magnificent even though their life cycle consumes only a single day. In the morning the bud springs open to release a pure white blossom. In early afternoon it transitions to a delicate pink. By evening its petals have darkened almost to a raspberry red. They then fold in upon themselves, and the darkness shuts them tight, never to open again. Each blossom uses the single day of its life to be a God-given parable of our earthly sojourn. As the ancient prophet reminded us, "surely the people are grass. The grass withers and the flowers fall, but the word of the Lord stands forever" (Isaiah 40:7, 8 NIV).

How I wish that Dorothy could be here before this bush once again. What a sweet time we would have merely looking at and commenting on these nine blossoms. But I cannot now speak with her about them or about anything else. I face what Edith Schaeffer first felt on receiving word of her mother's death: "the wall of separation" which death erects against any communication. With her I feel that same isolation in a separation so painful and so total that no one can get through. For me the distance is no longer a hideous "Berlin Wall," as at first. It does not dominate my thoughts and spoil every minute of my day. But there are moments it grabs my attention.

The impossibility of communication is real to me before my Confederate Rose bush. The conversation which once would have bound our hearts together cannot occur. Now it is for me to enjoy this moment and these flowers alone. And then move on into the autumn with my life and my memories.

31. Crossing the Goal Line

Approaching the one year anniversary of Dorothy's death, I sense how much my evaluation of both her life and death have changed. I have had nearly a full year to think back upon her accomplishments. Not until a human life is over can we start to trust our grasp of its meaning and value. Without her any longer at my side I now have the benefit both of the time and perspective to evaluate who she was and what she did. And this applies especially to our life together during the fifty-nine years of our marriage. Although it is an understatement, I can say with conviction that to the end Dorothy May Pierce was a good person to all and to me a loving and faithful wife.

Physical ills and trials made the last few years of our time together more difficult. We each were fairly healthy for the first seventy-five years of our lives. But since then our medical problems have multiplied, with mine seeming to be the more serious (like cancer, stroke, heart irregularities). Not as serious (but just as troubling for Dottie) a knee problem increasingly limiting her mobility. She feared that my pushing her in a wheel chair would become too hard for me. I recognized that her strength and endurance, both physically and emotionally, were diminishing. She found it increasingly difficult to prepare meals and complete her home keeping duties. We both acknowledged that we were entering the days of our marriage that really counted. We could still care for ourselves and each other; but we began to wonder for how much longer.

In discussing that uncertainty we both purposed to care for each other as long as we could. This was simply to keep our promise to be "loving and faithful ... in plenty and in want, in joy and in sorrow, in sickness and in health, 'til death do us part.'" Now in our closing years we would have the opportunity to live out our promises. We found ourselves discussing our intentions in the football terminology of nearing the "goal line" and approaching "pay dirt." God was bringing us near this important time when it would require serious effort to express the love God had given us. The infatuation and romance of our youth would not have been adequate. The times now demanded the mature devotion of two individuals united in caring for each other as long as they lived.

This dedication to serve one another was nothing new. We had intended it from the beginning of our life together. And in spite of our imperfections we tried to keep it as a guiding principle of our marriage. We were determined to keep our wedding vows.

So on a Monday in October, 2010 she traveled with me to Gainesville, Florida so that I could receive an atrial ablation, a surgical procedure under anesthesia to correct irregularities in my heart rhythm. She waited for my return from the operating room, brought me home and cared for me as I recuperated. Neither of us knew how close we were to the

"goal line" and "pay dirt." Only two days later she was be-
set by a weakness she had never known before. It would
claim her life in less than two weeks. But before that it
would be my turn to lift her in and out of bed, to prepare
her meals, to move her in a wheel chair, to transport her to
a hospital, to make decisions about her treatment, to arrange for her maximum comfort, and to be at her side when
she died. To be without her is the greatest sorrow of my
life. And yet the pain is tempered by my satisfaction in
knowing we had reached "pay dirt" together. Our marriage
had crossed the "goal line" and we both had kept our promises to God and to each other. She cared for me until her
weakness made it impossible; then I took care of her. With
God's help we cared for one another until death separated
us. This consolation means more to me with each passing
day. She cared for me with the last measure of her declining
strength; and I was able to minister to her needs in her final
days. To the end, she was faithful to me; and I was to her.
Just as we had promised before God.

I like to think that God answered for Dorothy and me
the closing requests in Dr. Louis H. Evans' *Prayer for a
Bride and Groom*: "When life is done and the sun is setting, may they be found then as now hand in hand, still
thanking God for each other, May they serve Thee happily,
faithfully, together until at last one shall lay the other into
the arms of God."

Other circumstances might have changed the details,
but when Dorothy and I crossed the goal line together it
was I who had the privilege of committing her into the
arms of the Lord. It was a precious privilege indeed.

32. Today Was the Day

Today I took off my wedding ring.

Let me be the first to admit that I should have done so long before this. Dorothy died a year ago this week, and so I can't claim that I haven't had the time to do it before now. In the early days of my being alone, to be honest with you, I didn't think much about the matter at all. I was just too busy with other pressing duties, like making arrangements for the funeral or spending time with family members who arrived to share our sorrow together. Following the service and their departures for home, legal papers required my attention. Then responsibilities like notifying people of her death, or writing "Thank you" notes, paying bills, and rearranging my home.

Before things quieted down I became aware that the ring was still on my finger and made several feeble attempts to remove it; but my knuckle proved too big an obstacle. I'm afraid that my efforts were half-hearted at best. I put the task aside with the observation that I had too much arthritis in my knuckle for me to succeed. The ring would probably have to be cut off and that procedure could wait. Then I pretty much forgot it was still there.

Looking back, I suspect that I didn't want to take the ring off. Dottie had put it on my finger on a humid summer day in June, 1951 amidst all the excitement of starting our life together. Even though I was painfully aware that our marriage had come to its end when she died, I still love her—perhaps even more than I did then. Seeing that ring on my left hand helped me to remember the years that we had shared together. Deep inside me I had no real desire to take it off. Yet in recent weeks as the anniversary of her death approached my feelings began to change.

Maybe I have become more concerned about what people might be thinking. After all, my wedding ring tells them that I am married. Which is true no longer. So why do I continue to wear the ring?

Will people think that I refuse to accept the reality that I am now a widower? (That's still an awkward word to me.) I may continue to find that term uncomfortable; yet I have accepted the reality that I am no longer a married man. Indeed, I am reconciled to my new status.

Subtly, my thoughts were moving beyond the symbolism of the ring itself. I was beginning to consider the meaning of the very act of removing a wedding ring. What would it be saying for me to take it off my finger? Certainly doing so would not signify that I was repudiating the precious privilege of having been married. It would not be like a divorce! No, but it would be a deliberate and conscious acknowledgment of the end of a cherished relationship.

My marriage did not end by the choice of either of us. That was the last thing that either Dottie or I wanted. But God in his providence did bring our marriage to an end. I accepted that reality at the time it happened. With great sorrow, yes; but without anger or bitterness. Why should I not let people know that? I have accepted the end of my marriage as God's plan for Dottie and me at that point in our lives. The right time had come for me to act. I removed my wedding ring today.

It didn't come off easily. I soaked my hand in ice water (as someone had suggested) and then tried unsuccessfully to push and pull the skin under the ring. Next I applied liquid soap around it, only to find the ring was too slippery to get a firm grip on it. My enlarged knuckle resisted the attempts. It took another ice bath with more pushing, pulling and twisting before my ring finally worked free.

I held it in my hand and acknowledged that my marriage is over. If I wept and struggled to control my feelings, you can appreciate why. The day my marriage ended was the saddest day of my life. The hurt is still real. Several times in the past I had taken off my wedding ring (once for a jeweler to repair it; again as I was preparing for surgery). No tears then. But today when I removed the ring I was doing so for one final time.

After doing so, I sensed that I had taken a decisive step, one far more significant than I could ever have guessed. I was thanking God for the past, I was accepting his will for my life at this time, and I was ready not to forget but to go forward with confidence that God wanted me to live again.

On this occasion I placed the golden circle on the palm of my hand. It glistened there as brightly as when Dottie first put it on my finger. I could almost relive the excitement, happiness and hopes of my wedding day. I was surprised at how beautifully the bumps and scratches of the years had polished its surface. Just as the hard times we shared had enriched our marriage. I gazed on its luster for a fitting length of time and reviewed again the life God gave me with Dorothy. How wonderful to know that we had both kept the promises we exchanged when she made that gift to me.

And now I have entrusted my wedding ring to a drawer already containing other items bearing treasured memories. I will revisit this token of Dottie's love for me again. In the meantime, I feel sure that in removing my wedding ring I have expressed my full faith in the verse God provided me at the beginning of my sorrow: "The Lord gave and the Lord has taken away; may the name of the Lord be praised" (Job 1:21 NIV).

Part Five

Two Final Letters

*T*hose who pick up the pen (or peck away on a word processor) have no guarantee that anyone will ever read what they write. That doesn't keep me from hoping that someone may read this volume and even persevere to this point. For the benefit of anyone who does so I enclose two letters.

My first letter is for you, my reader. I could not identify any particular point in my story where its content would fit comfortably. Yet, I was certain that it contained important facts for you to know. My letter is a simple explanation of the beliefs that have shaped my time of sorrow. It's not an apologetic for what I believe, nor a polemic to attack anyone who might differ with me. I think that it will enlighten you about my experience of grief.

The second letter is to my wife. I still have times when I want to tell Dorothy about . . ." And that's the case today. (In the past, I would have asked her judgment on illustrations, quotations, even whole chapters. But she doesn't know anything about this book.) If she were still here with me, this is what I would like her to know.

Will you read this letter for Dottie?

33. To My Readers

Dear Reader,

These pages record my struggle to understand what
happens to a grieving person. My confusion over what was
going on in my own life prompted me to write them. Sadness takes its place beside joy, love, surprise, desire, anger
and fear as a universal human emotion. All who live long
enough will face grief. At the same time, feeling sad is also
a unique experience, different for each person. On one
hand, you may immediately identify with me because you
have already experienced some of what I have gone
through. At the same time, you may be mystified by some
of my reactions. They will strike you as strange.

Don't worry! I've felt puzzled by them, too. Sorrow
does affect each of us differently, and not always in the way
we expect. Our personalities, experiences, feelings for the
person we mourn, and beliefs about life and death—these
may all differ significantly. We can't explore all of these in-
fluences, but I do need to bring together for you my personal views about the nature of life and death.

Long before sorrow disrupted my life I had thought seriously about these matters. And I doubt that anyone can assess how I have grieved apart from knowing something about my conclusions. My beliefs were formed years ago and are still with me.

Don't worry if you yourself see things differently. I'm not trying to change you. I just want to share with you my beliefs about death. They have influenced me deeply since Dottie died. Knowing them should better enable you to evaluate how my beliefs may have framed my experience of sorrow.

I believe that during the previous year God was preparing me for the end of our time together, and doing so by building upon my lifelong relationship to him. I began to cultivate that friendship with God during my high school years and have since attempted to understand myself and my world in the light of what the Bible says. In that book I met an almighty and loving God, creator of an originally perfect world, but one which has subsequently been marred by sin. The result has surrounded us with decay, disease and death. However, these defects need not have the last word because God has acted in history to restore his creation to its original perfection. He sent Jesus to do this through his own life, death and resurrection. As a result Jesus has promised his followers that "because I live, you will live also" (John 14:19). Though they too will die, those who believe in him look forward to receiving the eternal life he has promised.

Between now and then I believe God wants us to take two things seriously: the sorrowful reality of death, and the

comforting awareness of his presence with those who remain. Death is unavoidable in our world where "It is ap-
pointed unto men once to die" (Heb 9:27 KJV). We should
not deny   death's existence, but acknowledge it for what it
is: the enemy which terminates human life. At the same
time, we know that Christ has already defeated this adver-
sary by his resurrection from the grave. As Adam's de-
scendants we must die bodily; but as believers in Christ we
shall rise bodily. Thus God points us to our "blessed hope"
(Titus 2:13), the return of Christ which brings about our
resurrection.

Of the several different ways in which Scripture speaks
of death, I have been helped most by its frequent use of
sleep as a synonym for a person's death. (The King James
Version, with which I grew up, employs some form of this
term about seventy times.) 'Sleep" is the Bible's usual way
of describing death, and agrees with our everyday use of
the word death to mean "the cessation, or the resulting absence, of life." Like ordinary sleep, death is a period of inactivity and unconsciousness. In agreement with this,
Scripture says that the righteous who die "rest from their labors" (Rev 14:13) and that they "sleep in Jesus" (1 Thess
4:14). Believers remain dead until they "awaken" in the
resurrection at Christ's Second Coming (1 Cor 15:20-23).
Here and elsewhere, the Bible contrasts death with life.

In Scripture death is not "life somewhere else," nor is it
another "more (or less) desirable form of life." Put simply,
death is the opposite of life. It is not death, but resurrection,
which provides our hope. Death takes away life; resurrection restores it. This Christians express in the words of the
Apostle's Creed: "I believe . . . in the resurrection of the

body." Resurrection enables Christians (both living and dead) to reunite with one another, following which they "will be with the Lord forever" (1 Thess 4:17). Meanwhile, when someone I love dies, I am not left alone for the God of all comfort has promised "I will never leave you, nor forsake you" (Heb 13:5, ESV). (In passing, let me share that I have found God's personal presence with me to be my greatest source of comfort.)

So I do not consider that physical death is the end. I rest on God's promise to raise believers from the grave and grant them the fullness of eternal life in the last day. Meanwhile, the death of any person remains a serious matter. I do not rejoice when people die. Death is not anybody's friend. It ends our earthly life and separates us from the ones we love. Christ will destroy this enemy death at the last (1 Cor 15:26). In the meantime I rest in the confidence that believers who die "have fallen asleep in Christ" (1 Cor 15:17) and will awaken in the resurrection of the last day (1 Cor 15:51-52)

The next conscious moment for the believer who dies will bring the joy of reunion with Christ and other loved ones. My hope as a Christian is not death, but the promised resurrection when the believer arises with a sinless, glorified, healthy resurrection body.

You may be surprised at how frequently I use the words death or die. I do not like the terms, but they do depict accurately what happened to my wife. She died. I avoid euphemisms designed to ease the pain of her absence. I do not say "she passed away," or that she has "gone to heaven," or that I "lost her" (although that last phrase sometimes sneaks in). I try to employ the biblical terminology.

I now grieve because she has died; but I do expect to rejoice when she rises from the dead. In the meantime, I also expect to know the comfort of God's personal presence with me.

These thoughts about God, death and resurrection (what people normally call *theology*) have provided the framework for my thinking about what has been happening to me during these trying days. My experience has given me no reason to doubt what I find in the Bible. These pages should display how these Bible teachings have helped me to keep my balance when my world seemed to collapse around me. And I hope that this explanation of my beliefs will throw light for you on my particular experience of grief. I have found the Bible to be what it claims to be: "A lamp to my feet and a light for my path" (Ps 119:105). I do not know how I could have coped with sorrow's depressing pathway apart from my personal faith in God and his Word. I do not hesitate to commend it to you.

Thanks for listening to what has guided me through my grief,

David A. Dean

34. Closing Words to My Wife

My dearest Dorothy,

I know that you will not be able to read these words. But they express what I would like to tell you if you could.

I have been writing about you and me for much of the past year. And now the writing, rewriting, weeping, editing, and proofreading are almost over. Doing this has refreshed precious memories of our life together, brought you to life again in my heart, and encouraged me anew to be the man you could be proud of.

For the first three months, I was too emotionally upset to compose much. But as winter drew to a close, I could see and think more clearly and found many incidents to record and evaluate.

But as the first anniversary of your death drew near I realized that I was encountering fewer notable happenings and had less urge to write. The Lord had been healing my broken heart. The book was over. I will miss contemplating almost daily how much you have meant to me and how much I miss you.

By the way, when writing I did try to call you "Dottie" (as you preferred); but habits die hard and occasionally I have slipped back into writing about "Dorothy" (the name I like best). I know you will forgive me. Hopefully it should at least reduce the repetition.

When you died, I had no idea what my own experience of grief would feel like. I wished that I could have had access to some widower's account of his sorrow. Like a kind of road map to guide my steps. These records may exist; but I didn't have any at hand. So I took someone's advice to record my own experiences and reactions. Writing about such incidents did help me to gain a clearer picture of my trials and to cope better. That's when the idea of assembling these short articles into a volume came up. Maybe together they could provide some other man the guidance I had wished for.

Now that I'm almost through, I do think that a number of my experiences might help other mourners. If these accounts do make it easier for any fellow travelers then I will consider myself richly blessed. At the same time, I realize that each of us must travel a personal route. Some—but not all—of my trials will be familiar to others who sorrow. Yet each person will encounter unique burdens, quite distinct from mine. I hope that others may discern in what I have gone through at least contours of the terrain of sadness.

In a way, this whole book exposes what I have learned. But some things stand out for me. The first is about what I call my "grief attacks." I guess I had assumed that sorrow would lie on me like a wet blanket pressing in from all sides and overshadowing me all the time.

That has not been my experience. Rather, grief has ambushed me like a band of guerillas attacking an army patrol. It has taken advantage of incidental reminders to overwhelm me by surprise with a sense of unbearable pain and loss. My grief attacks have had specific causes: a special memory, or photograph, or sound—any reminder of our life together. They vary in frequency, intensity, and length; but usually they are unpredictable and arrive when I least expect them. I am rendered speechless, bewildered, distraught. My worst sorrow has not been steady or consistent, but has come unexpectedly and then left on its own timing.

A second lesson I have learned is that every memory has two sides. The first side of each memory of you is unbearably sad. It emphasizes my loss and intensifies my sense of being alone. It nudges me towards despair and urges me to banish you from my mind. But if I can only withstand the pain, a blessing awaits me. If I force my way through the initial sadness another side of the memory awaits. This aspect is as sweet as the first is bitter. It consists of beautiful and treasured moments (often long forgotten) when you enriched my life and gave it value. The second side of a memory only comes to mind when I search for it in the midst of my pain.

The first side of a memory is my sense of loss that you are not in my bed; but, the other side is the joy of recalling the intimacy of our mid-night conversations in India. I've learned that when I push through to this other side of my memories then I am able to reclaim you in a new way.

Let me mention a third lesson. The Lord has promised never to leave nor forsake us, and he never does. You came into my life, made it worth living, but then you had to leave. (How ironic, that we both expected me to go first.) But the same God who kept us when we were together has been with me since we parted. Even when I have almost let my sorrow block him out, God has come to reveal his love and energize my hope of a future reunion. I assured you he would care for you if I died first; I want to reassure you that God has done that for me. I hope that this record of my experience may confirm Jesus' promise, "Blessed are those who mourn, for they shall be comforted" (Matt 5:4 ESV).

It surprises me that what I have written is not what I thought I was composing. I intended to record my heartache and suffering. Yet in reviewing my story I discover that it actually is more about how the Lord has been with me, to lighten my load and to give me his comforting peace. These pages are not about my need, but about God's presence and provision. They are about a grief that is good because the Lord has been in it.

My fourth lesson is a theme that runs unspoken all through what I have written. During my months of sorrow, I have improved and my desire to live has returned. Time does heal. Yet, as Oswald Chambers once cautioned, it is really God, our loving Father who is "the great healer and consoler." He alone is "the God of all comfort, who comforts us in all our affliction" (2 Cor 1:3,4 ESV). I have found God's comfort to be constant even when its effect has been almost unseen. With time I hurt less and sorrow loses its power to cripple my life. Grief attacks become less frequent, less painful and shorter.

My path has not been easy. I am blessed that you have not had to tread it. Yet, though our separation is real, we remain united in that we are both in God's keeping. Whatever sorrow I may yet encounter God will still be my comfort. He who gave you to me now has taken you away; I will still praise his Name

Meanwhile, my dear, sleep well. I still love you and miss you so much. You have been God's greatest earthly gift to me. And I rest in his promise that we shall rejoin one another in a glorious resurrection morning when once again I will be . . .

Your Dave